EIGEN IN SEOUL:
VOLUME ONE,
MADNESS AND MURDER

EIGEN IN SEOUL: VOLUME ONE, MADNESS AND MURDER

Michael Eigen

Taylor & Francis Group

LONDON AND NEW YORK

First published 2010 by Karnac Books Ltd

Published 2018 by Routledge
2 Park Square, Milton Park, Abingdon, Oxon OX14 4RN
711 Third Avenue, New York, NY10017, USA

Routledge is an imprint of the Taylor & Francis Group, an informa business

Copyright © 2010 by Michael Eigen

The right of Michael Eigen to be identified as the authors of this work has been asserted in accordance with §§ 77 and 78 of the Copyright Design and Patents Act 1988.

All rights reserved. No part of this book may be reprint or reproduced or utilised in any form or by any electronic, mechanical, or other means, now known or hereafter invented, including photocopying and recording, or in any information storage or retrieval system, without permission in writing from the publishers.

Notice:
Product or corporate names may be trademarks or registered trademarks, and are use only for identification and explanation without intent to infrige.

British Library Cataloguing in Publication Data

A C.I.P. for this book is available from the British Library

ISBN-13: 978-1-85575-819-3 (pbk)

Typeset by Vikatan Publishing Solutions (P) Ltd., Chennai, India

CONTENTS

PREFACE   vii

CHAPTER ONE
Day 1   1

CHAPTER TWO
Day 2   21

CHAPTER THREE
Day 3   55

REFERENCES   91

PREFACE

These seminars were given in Seoul, 2007, on three consecutive days, six hours per day, a total of eighteen hours. Another set, not yet fully transcribed, took place two years later. It was a wonderful experience. Part of what made it wonderful was the chance to dig into the material in an intense, concentrated way with a very attuned and helpful group.

I began speaking about madness in psychoanalysis, showing how important psychosis was for Freud, Klein, Bion and Winnicott. It is a theme I opened up in my first book, *The Psychotic Core* in 1986 (republished by Karnac Books, 2004) and felt privileged to be able to enrich it with learning and experience twenty-one years later.

They say there are no atheists in foxholes. A tantalizing trait of human nature is our ability to exaggerate in order to convey the truth of emotional experience. It is an amazing trait, linked with imagination and the need to communicate, a need to share what is there. Whether or not there are no atheists in foxholes, we know in an immediate way what is meant. We share a sense of the horror, terror, damage and loss such a statement conveys.

In a parallel way, work with madness and trauma requires faith. A faith allied with skill and caring. Faith in what? It is hard to say.

There are many breeds of faith. Perhaps there is something we might call psychoanalytic or psychotherapeutic faith. Faith in being together, that in being together something good will happen.

Faith has many tributaries and links with art, music and spiritual experience, as well as science and skill. Psychoanalytic perception and sensing is creative. Contact with the unknown is enlivening. Psychoanalytic inspiration contributes to creative living in those it touches.

This seminar conveys something of the therapeutic faith, creativity, learning, and skill shared by Seoul therapists and myself. We confronted social, familial and individual ills, ills of the human condition. We shared cases, dilemmas in our lives, dilemmas in our societies, our world. We explored the riches of psychoanalytic psychotherapy, what it contributes to ourselves, to people we work with, to the world at large.

Perhaps most surprising to me was how simpatico we were together, people from across the world, who never met. We quickly found deep meeting points and appreciation for mutual aliveness that continues to grow.

I want to thank my translator and transcriber, Joon ho Lee, himself a student of psychoanalysis in the Boston Graduate School of Psychoanalysis. His feeling for psychoanalysis and the tone and spirit of my remarks made it possible for the "feel" of what I was saying, as well as content, to come through. Our "voices" worked together.

Many thanks to Betty Eigen, my partner, who worked out rough patches and problems in the transcribed manuscript, helping to make it more readable.

The seminar was sponsored by the Object Relations Institute for Psychoanalysis in Seoul, founded by Jae hoon Lee, who provided many nourishing moments for my family and myself and was a superb overseer of this meeting. Psychoanalysis is alive and well in Seoul. Not without growing pains, of course. But what I found was a group of dedicated seekers, open and caring, in touch with the pain and love of life, eager to do well by those in their charge. Eager to do right by the depths of their own existence. I hope these pages convey something of the richness of our experience.

Michael Eigen
January 2010, New York City

CHAPTER ONE

Day 1

Madness in psychoanalysis: Freud and Klein

First let me get the feel of the microphone. Is the sound OK? I was told that there are some twenty art therapists here. My wife is an art therapist in addition to being a more general child and adult therapist. So I'm happy to welcome art therapists and everyone else.

I was saying earlier today that I'm happy if in a meeting one sentence or one phrase that I manage to utter is significant to one person. If that happens I will be happy and if more than that happens even better. Meaning is very hard to transmit. Meaning is very hard to communicate and there is so much noise in our psychic systems, in our heads, in our souls, that it is very hard to understand each other, certainly even to understand ourselves, but we'll give it a try. I welcome the chance to communicate with you, or try to, and for you to communicate with me.

I'm going to speak about madness in psychoanalysis. There will be time for questions, for responses, for your thoughts and feelings. I like interruptions so feel free to interrupt me anytime about anything as the spirit moves you. Nothing I'm saying is so important that it can't be interrupted. Maybe the interruption will be much more important. We don't know. So I will talk but if you don't interrupt me, I'll just keep on talking.

I'm going to talk about madness in psychoanalysis and I'm going to begin with Freud. Most of what I am saying today in this first session will be about Melanie Klein but I want to pave the way by beginning with Freud. Madness was very important from the beginning of psychoanalysis. Freud's formal or official theory is about neuroses. But if you look closely and examine the concepts he uses, he draws his main concepts from a phenomenology of psychoses. The concepts he uses are drawn from experience of psychosis, which he applies to the neuroses and cultural phenomena.

Freud spent time in a mental hospital not as a patient but with other doctors. He was exposed to psychotic behaviour and learned a lot about psychosis from poets and from his own self. I write about this extensively in my first book, *The Psychotic Core*. If any of you get the urge to take a look at it, you will see some of this material there. Look at his concepts. For example the id. The id is portrayed as quite mad: the law of contradiction does not hold, common sense does not hold, and space and time collapse, reverse, turn inside out. In a way, Freud poeticized aspects of the id (The It), romanticized aspects of madness in the id.

The link between psychosis and Freud's ego is a little harder to see, but I will point it out. Before moving on to the ego, my thoughts just interrupted themselves, so I'm going to share the interruption. At the end of Freud's life, in one of the last notes he wrote, he commented that mysticism is the ego's perception of the id. I was thinking, after I told you that the id has various structures of madness, that many of these structures are also true of mystical experience. Common sense may not hold, the law of contradiction doesn't hold, space and time are transcended and have different laws and so on. So there seems to be some resonance between Freud's depiction of the psychotic id and Freud's association of that with mystical experience. I'm not going to reduce one to the other. I'm just noting an affinity that appeared in his work.

For Freud the ego begins quite mad. He says that the ego begins as a hallucinatory organ and that the first cognitions are hallucinatory. The early (and not so early) ego moves in and out of hallucination. Hallucination is one of its modes of cognition. Associated with this is the thought that the ego is a wish-fulfilling organ. It hallucinates fulfillment of wishes.

As a hallucinating wish-fulfilling organ, the ego can temporarily hallucinate pain away, hallucinate pain as not there, and substitute pleasure where there is pain. The ego overcomes distress by hallucinating it not there and hallucinating bliss or pleasure or a heavenly, beatific state as there. In this "madness" of the ego early in life, there is a double hallucination, a negative hallucination and a positive one. Negative hallucination: hallucinating something there, as not there e.g., hallucinating pain away. Positive hallucination: hallucinating something not there as there, e.g., hallucinating bliss when there is distress.

Freud creates an example, a thought experiment, a psychoanalytic fantasy: when the baby is hungry, the baby hallucinates a breast as there. Insofar as the baby lacks clear time perspective hunger may feel boundless, distress without end. The baby doesn't know that soon the hunger will be satisfied and the distress will end. For the moment, distress goes on forever, infinitely, hellishly. Freud imagines the baby hallucinating a breast; a fulfilling feed to stop the fear and agony for a time. The baby substitutes an imaginary feed in his mind to quell very real distress, very real hunger. A propensity to make believe and substitute fantasy for reality begins.

This is one way the human race is crazy—a fundamental tendency, according to Freud, to believe that one's desires are fulfilled in order to make the pain of unfulfillment disappear. To take this farther, saying it a little differently, we become used to making ourselves disappear in order to survive ourselves. We make aspects of ourselves disappear in order to endure living with ourselves. We are self-disappearing creatures.

This is not the whole truth about our nature and who we are. It is but one tendency, but an important one. If we don't catch on to it, feel our way into it, taste, smell and live with it, then it is going to come at us from outside. If we don't catch onto our self-disappearing nature from the inside, it will come at us from outside. We will make ourselves disappear from the outside, by what we do to each other and to the world. So much human violence is an attempt to make this fact about ourselves clear to us. Unfortunately, we obliterate this information by mechanisms like blame, as if blaming will make the pain go away. Blame is often part of wish fulfillment. We point to sources of violence out there and miss the internal mechanism that disappears us. Outer violence is important as a source of pain but we must not allow it to blot out ways we disappear ourselves because of inherent pain. It's almost as if aliveness is too much for us. It's too much to be alive. We can't endure the pain we go through. We can't take the full intensity of our feelings. Freud spoke of primal trauma as flooding. Flooded by intense feeling. Waves of feeling, we say, and they appear in dreams of drowning. We disperse, drown, and go dead in face of feelings that are more than we can take. We get flooded by the rise and fall of experience and go under.

What does a baby do when experience gets too rough, after screaming? He stupors out, goes into a trance, goes to sleep, loses consciousness. We do this too in our own ways as adults. How we make ourselves, our feelings, aspects of inner reality disappear in face of painful intensity is a happening that requires recognition and reflection. To make ourselves disappear, to make pain disappear, is a mad state. It occludes or obliterates aspects of reality, inner and outer. The ego in such moments is an unreality machine.

You'll find out in the next three days that I don't really expect you or me to do anything about such states. Its best not to try to do too much. But it's good to develop what I call psychic taste buds, to taste the psyche and psychic processes, smell it, taste it, feel it. Don't try to make it go away. Try to taste a little bit more of it, live your way into it and see what happens.

As the ego goes on, for Freud, it develops socialized ways of living with self disappearing as a way of handling aliveness, a way of handling stimulation it can't bear. One of the best portrayals he has of this is in his book *Group Psychology and the Analysis of the Ego* (1921). There he talks about transference and idealization. Particularly idealizing authority figures—parent, teacher, religion, nation, whatever. He talks about self-idealization and he talks about idealization of different groups. And he sees in idealization the working of hallucinatory processes through which one tries to escape the pain. I personally find many positive things in our idealizing tendency. So I'm not cancelling it or putting it down or making it disappear. It is very real and we have to learn to live with it like we learn to live with breathing. But we also have to see how it is a cocoon for hidden madness and hidden pain.

Now Freud performs a magician's trick, a sleight of hand. He says that the ego, while starting out psychotic, is a double agent because it is also involved with the perception of reality. It has a double capacity. It has hallucinatory origins and also is dedicated to perceiving reality. It's almost as if Freud is asking the question, 'How does a hallucinogenic organ develop anti-hallucinogenic properties?' He doesn't solve this. No one has ever really solved this, at least not in the terms it has been asked. But from another point of view, Freud is honoring a double capacity we have, although our ways of talking about it leave much to be desired.

When Freud was younger, he developed his theory of sexuality and libido. He was very into the experience of vitality. When he was older he developed a theory about a destructive drive, Thanatos, a death drive. When he was younger the life drive carried the aggression in the personality. The life drive wasn't sweet and meek. The life drive was hungry. The life drive was acquisitive, aggressive and ambitious. It was driven. The ego was driven by a hunger for life. It wasn't a sweet and withdrawn thing. It sought to maximize life. And we know from human history that the life drive kills. One kills out of the life drive. Give me yours. I want yours. I want to take your part of life and add it to mine. So the life drive is highly dangerous. There is really not much to check it. The ego doesn't do a terribly good job in the course of history knowing what to do with the fact that we are killers and that our life drive is dangerous. Some of us try to withdraw from it, play it down, tone it down. And it becomes a question of how much life we can stand and how to begin modulating it. To begin somehow finding a way to not be so alive. Tone it down a little. Be a little more dead. Deaden the life drive because it will kill us. The life drive will kill us. It will kill others. It will kill us in our desirous hungry modes. So we try to develop a trade-off, a compromise with life, so that we can get through it, live it. In order to live the life drive we have to kill it a little bit.

Now as he got older and near the end of his life, he lived through the First World War and the Second World War was on the horizon, he had to leave his country. He had no idea just how horrible things were going to be, but he already had a glimpse. He had the death of a daughter and he had cancer. And he began to wonder more about certain patients who didn't change in the way he thought they should. He tried to stay with the libido theory. Maybe the libido is too sticky. Maybe the libido is too inert. Maybe there is something wrong with the libido. Eventually he had to add what he called the destructive drive, the death drive. A drive that tends toward disappearing, making the human creature go back to inorganic life. A drive that can't support the tensions of life, that must undo the conflicts, tensions, the irascibility of life, and tend back toward zero.

Now we know that there are many problems with the death drive as a biological theory, and I wouldn't present it as that. And maybe even the death drive is part of the life drive. That's also possible. But as a description, as a poetic description, as a majestic description of human self-destruction, it's like a notation; it's like a flag. It says, "Look at this. Something is going on here." Maybe this isn't the best way to talk about it, but we've got to talk about it some way because it is lethal and it is us.

So far I've presented aspects of Freud's concepts of the id and the ego, which are permeated by some kind of madness. I haven't mentioned the superego because most analysts understand that the superego goes mad very easily and over-persecutes the rest of the personality. It's as if the destructiveness of the id or the ego gets recycled through the superego and then re-channeled against the ego and the id. So that an overly ambitious destructive persecutory superego is aimed at the rest of the personality and is quite mad. What I'm trying to bring out is not only that the superego is mad, or the id is mad, but that the ego is mad too. All three of Freud's main structures are permeated with threads that are on a psychotic level.

I'm beginning by painting this grim picture because it is too easy to think that Freud simply says "Oh we have to compromise, we have to think about reality, we have to live our sane common sense or logic." Because in the depths of his theory sanity can be mad or tinged with madness. What seems sane to one group is insane to another group and hostility between groups is rationalized by 'My way is right and your way is wrong.' Institutionalized murder, as in war or execution of supposed criminals, operates under a cloak of "sanity."

Now we will begin Melanie Klein. Melanie Klein (1946, 1957) picks up where Freud's death drive left off. She is a death drive analyst and her concepts developed within a cultural context of warfare. Her picture of the psyche is a war psychology. It's a psychology concerned with a destructive drive, what she calls a destructive urge within. Mystical Judaism speaks of a good inclination and an evil inclination, and Melanie Klein's analysis focuses very much on the evil inclination, on our destructive drive. She also makes explicit what's implicit in Freud. She taps the concern with madness that's implicitly hidden in Freud's concept. It's all there like fools gold on the surface. You just have to see it, like the purloined letter—all of the madness that's in Freud. It's almost as if he changed the discourse from focusing on sin to focusing on madness. But in Melanie Klein it becomes explicit. Because her psychology is explicitly about psychotic conflicts and psychotic agonies. I think it's the first systematic, so to speak, systematic/unsystematic psychoanalytic psychology that focuses solely—no, that's not quite true—I'm omitting Federn (see Eigen, 1986). Federn was probably the first and we're leaving him out. But no one has focused on the destructive drive in psychotic conflict as fiercely as Klein has.

When Klein started speaking about psychotic conflicts, psychotic agony, she released a stream of creative writers to begin talking about psychosis. Bion's work, Winnicott's work, Andre Green's work, Marion Milner's work all have Klein in the background. And they disagree this way or that way with Klein. But it's as if once she says it, once she taps it, it opens up energy that had been bottled up and one begins to see, one begins to contact, one begins to perceive and envision all sorts of ways that madness works.

At the center of her theory is a simple dynamic vision or observation or imagining or taste that fits in with aspects of existential psychology. She feels that the core psychotic anxiety is annihilation, annihilation anxiety. She calls it annihilation dread. And it spans many levels. For her it is quite physical. It's in the body but it's also mental. It's a fear of loss of mind, a fear of loss of self, a psychical annihilation as well as a physical annihilation. With a little introspection, some of you know that psychic annihilation is much more dreadful than physical annihilation. She began talking about annihilation dread and psychotic ways of handling it, responding to it.

She envisioned two main ways to go crazy. In all cultures, in all times, people have gone crazy either by being what we call schizophrenic or what we call depressed. She noted that these two ways of going crazy are also ways of defending against annihilation anxiety. It's as if one goes crazy in order to avoid being annihilated. She took those two ways of going crazy and turned them into defenses. What she calls the paranoid-schizoid style or mode or position is one way of dealing with psychotic anxiety, annihilation anxiety, and the depressive position is another. She took the two main ways that people go crazy and turned them into psychoanalytic defenses, ways of handling conflicts over annihilation anxiety.

Now each of these two positions or modes of handling annihilation anxiety are made up of many complex processes, micro processes, and Melanie Klein hit on a few of them. She elaborated aspects of Freud's thinking about how the ego works. In the paranoid-schizoid position, she saw the ego try to rid itself of pain by putting it somewhere else, e.g., putting one's own pain in the other person or in empty space, getting the pain outside the self. The usual way it does this is by projecting it into the other. In the United States a lot of people do not like the term projective identification. It may be an awkward term, but touches an important reality. That is, we are identified with what we project. We might try to get rid of painful elements by putting them in someone else, but we are unconsciously identified with them. Our identity is hooked up with what we put into others. We don't get rid of what we throw out of ourselves. We are deeply invested in it even if we try to kill it off out there. Then she notes that what you put into the other comes back to you, it boomerangs. You project out scary things, you see scary things. You project out nightmarish elements, you see nightmarish elements. And you become paranoid. You become more withdrawn. You try to hide from the monstrous formations, the painful formations you are trying to rid yourself of.

She speaks of splitting and idealization. Freud wrote that the ego idealizes authority figures, in part, to get rid of one's own psychic disturbances. Splitting, projection, idealization are ways to blunt disturbance, displace it, exile it. Besides splitting, projection and idealization, Klein also wrote about denial and manic defense. Those of you who read Kernberg will note that his descriptions of the borderline personality use the same defenses that for Klein are part of psychotic operations in face of annihilation anxiety.

It is interesting and I think important to note the strong role paranoid processes have played in both Freud's and Klein's thinking about psychotic states. Most of Freud's writings on psychosis were on paranoia. He classified psychosis into two categories: paranoia and everything else. For Freud, paranoia was extremely important in understanding the ego and Klein picked up on that. Klein's paranoid-schizoid mode of operation links in to the way the ego idealizes, hallucinates, splits and defends itself from pain, as described by Freud. The main pain for Klein is annihilation anxiety and her emphasis on the latter constitutes a shift in the center of gravity for psychoanalysis.

An interesting thing about Klein's use of splitting is that she uses it to explain deadness or unfeeling. If you keep on splitting in order to keep away annihilation anxiety and keep on splitting, the splitting proliferates a little like the sorcerer's apprentice. It proliferates and disperses the ego instead of saving the ego. Splitting tries to save some domain of the ego by dispersing it. The psyche gets dispersed and as the psyche gets dispersed, it thins out and loses contact and stops feeling itself. It's as if splitting carried far enough into dispersal leads to the loss of the capacity to feel oneself fully alive or fully present and one begins more and more to feel not there or dead or unfeeling.

The other mode depression, the depressive position, is a way of handling anxiety, persecutory anxiety, annihilation anxiety and Klein and Bion both talk about depression as persecutory. Depression is a self-persecutory mode of defending oneself. In the depressive position, Klein depicts the infant ego as solving annihilation anxiety by feeling itself as destructive, by feeling the id as destructive, i.e., a sense of myself and my basic feelings and drives as destructive. We solve psychic nebulae, psychic ambiguity by causal ideas. I did it, you did it. I'm the bad one. You're the bad one. It's a seesaw. We try to give some organization to annihilation anxiety by saying it's because of you I feel this, or it's because of me you feel that. We try to somehow circumscribe the work of this dumbfounding annihilation anxiety by giving it a causal form. And Melanie Klein's way of doing it is by having the baby say it's because of me mommy feels bad. It's sort of like a projection of the depression. It's at the mother. I'm making mom feel bad. Of course with some mothers at some times or all mothers at some times it's not a projection. The mother might really feel depressed, might be depressed, might feel bad and might blame the infant for it. That's a whole other thing. That's something else that we may get to. But right now I want to keep the focus on Klein's way of having the baby solve, get out of this annihilation anxiety by attributing causality to itself. Now instead of projecting it, it introjects it. I'm the one, I'm the monster. I bite the hand that feeds me. I'm to blame. It's preparing the way for shame, for guilt. And in this scheme indeed Klein depicts guilt as a higher form of development. It's not mother who is persecuting me, its me who is persecuting her. It's all my fault, and I have to make amends. I have to make up for it—what Klein calls reparation. I want to repair. I want to repair the damage that I caused. I want to make good. I want to make mom better and I want to feel good again. I want to feel that I'm not such a destructive being.

So I'm either projecting the destructiveness into the other, they are the bad ones, or I'm introjecting the badness into myself and feeling I'm the bad one. In either case it's a very circumscribed causal organization that runs from the more devastating fact that we don't know what to do with annihilation anxiety. It's there and we defend ourselves in natural ways through paranoia and depression by blaming the other or blaming ourselves. But the fact is in a larger panoramic view of ourselves we don't know what to do with our destructive impulses and with our annihilation dreads. We have not solved this and our solutions have led to great trouble. Of course it's produced civilizations, it's led to a lot of good things too. But at the present time it has led to the danger of our environment going under, of unending warfare for economic reasons, and I could go on and on with a litany of the splits, the social splits and the class splits and so on and so forth that we have not solved and don't know how to solve. And maybe when we talk about Bion later tomorrow, we will begin to realize how important it is to able to say, "I don't know how to do this. I don't know what is going on. I don't have an adequate approach to it. But I know something is happening and my solutions to it in the past have only worked in a very limited way and are causing great danger to the world now."

Just one more thing here. There is a great deal of fluidity between these two positions, between the paranoid-schizoid and depressive. So much so that people could diagnose a case either way. For example in the Freud Schreber case (1911), Freud diagnoses Schreber as suffering from paranoid dementia, a kind of paranoid schizophrenia, a paranoia. But there are other workers today, Zvi Lothane (1992), who diagnose Schreber as depressive, as bipolar. So it's hard to keep these domains separate. Now the traditional Kleinians try to keep them sort of separate by saying that the paranoid-schizoid is earlier and inferior and more primitive. And the depressive is more advanced, more human, healthier. But I suspect the reality is that if one looks at it that way one is going to be putting down elements in oneself for being inferior, and putting up elements in oneself for being superior, and being wrong in both cases. It will be a case of devaluing one and idealizing the other. So I wouldn't idealize the depressive position or the paranoid-schizoid position. I wouldn't assign one as better than the other at all because they are different forms of going crazy, or they are different forms of using what could be called crazy operations. Using it, channeling it, and doing something worthwhile is possible with either one.

There can be different kinds of splits in paranoia. For example, there is a split between love and hate. It could be that I feel love and I project the hate. So I don't feel the bad stuff. I feel the good stuff. Or it could be I feel the hate and I project the love. That's a simple split. This kind of split probably makes me feel more alive. It doesn't consciously make me feel more dead. If I'm hating or loving, I feel more alive.

But in the wider psychic field including the unconscious field, if I'm splitting even though I am feeling more alive by loving or hating, it's at a cost to the total psyche. It's at a cost to the total personality. I'm feeling more alive at the expense of losing part of myself. I'm feeling more alive but the price I pay is a shrunken identity, a smaller identity. I'm identified with my love or I'm identified with my hate consciously. But unconsciously I'm also identified with the opposite that I'm trying not to experience. Even while I'm feeling more alive consciously the psyche already is beginning to disappear, to die, to shrink, to whither, because it's not as full as it could be.

So in this case whether I love or whether I hate, I'm a shrunken smaller version of myself. Now I may not experience the deadness but the annihilation is there. I've paid a price for my aliveness and then I have to defend this aliveness. If something happens that threatens it, this small I, this alive I, I have to marshal my defenses and split off those threats one way or another. And the more I have to defend myself and the more splitting I have to do to get rid of the threats, the smaller and tighter and more contracted I become.

I become addicted to a pocket of aliveness, a pocket of identity and keep on splitting and splitting to defend that little piece. And that little piece seems to get smaller and smaller the more I try to defend it. Or it gets more and more inflated. In either case, it will reach a point where I will begin to feel the deadness either because the inflation disperses me, or the smallness and the contraction make me disappear.

So the more I try to defend myself the more the psyche gets dispersed. The more I try to fight to preserve my little I, my little I feeling, my little island of I feeling, my little aliveness, the psyche gets more and more dispersed to a point where I begin to feel the deadness all around and inside me and have to fight that off too.

Well I hope I didn't scare everybody off from speaking or asking questions or wanting more clarification. When I listen to questions and try to say something, I don't know if I'm responding to the right question or whether I understood the question or if my response is OK. Please tell me how you feel about my response and we can try again or if you don't feel I can do better we can give up. But we can try to do it better.

Question 1

I understood from your explanation that the ego starts from splitting and there are two ways in which it continues to split. If our goal in psychoanalysis is to prevent the psyche from dying and to have enough experience of feeling alive, is it possible to protect the ego and experience the psyche at the same time? Essentially, is it possible to protect the ego and at the same time experience the psyche or does one have to give up the ego in order to experience? I would like to know your thoughts.

Response 1

We can't experience the full psyche. We never will. We cannot give up the ego, at least most of us can't. We can try and try but it's probably not going to happen. We don't even know what the ego is. It's just a word. It's just an abstraction. We don't even know what we mean. We could say I, "I." We don't know if there are times we give that up, or if something else happens. But you know I would like to say this: That yes, Melanie Klein seems to begin with splitting and that is exactly where Winnicott and Bion disagree with her. Both Winnicott and Bion look towards other or even earlier or less clear processes for the beginning of psychic life. Even before the ego is formed enough to do something like split.

Even Freud had states, in a sense earlier than the ego, that sort of look like the ego. One of them he called reversal of affect, where one affect would turn into another. And for him that forms part of the background, part of the soil, in which the ego flowers. There are already processes going on before I become aware of "I", or "I" begins to take hold as an organization. Even in Freudian thinking there are background processes that precede the "I". For Freud the processes in which one affect turns into another, like love turning into hate or hate turning into love, he doesn't call splitting. Melanie Klein does begin with a kind of splitting but I don't think that Freud really does and I think she missed that. I think that there is a fluidity, a psychic fluidity prior to splitting that Klein missed. I wouldn't say that the ego begins with splitting if one can talk about the ego at this point. One can say that the ego has much more fluidity before it organizes a firm paranoid defense.

Actually Freud did say that we don't give up anything. That was his view. His official view is that we are incapable of giving up anything. But my own feeling is that we should stop trying to give up things. It is only going to cause more needless struggle, more needless suffering. I think it is better to sit and taste, taste this, taste that. Make room for this, make room for that. Get to know this, get to know that. Not to make so many decisions ahead of time about what to keep and what to give up because we don't really know what we are messing around with. And it's good to just sit there and take a taste and keep tasting.

Question 2

There is one thing that I felt internally and one question I had. The feeling I had was that in order to protect ourselves from the harsh and uncertain reality we all have an adaptive madness and this was moving. I used to work at a mental hospital in which many patients were diagnosed with psychotic depression or schizophrenia and the doctors used to teach that they were originally psychotic. In other words, they told us not to empathize with their severe symptoms. But if we view madness as a part of us that we all share, then I do not have to give up on trying to empathize and connect with the patients because they share something in me that only looks a little bit different, and this was very touching for me. Second, my question is about the paranoid-schizoid and depressive position and what you said about one not being inferior or superior that the other. Many theorists, including David Scharff, talk about the treatment process and how the patient moves on to the depressive position when there is progress and how he regresses to the paranoid-schizoid position when something has gone bad in the treatment. If there is no one position better than the other. Dr. Eigen, what would the clinical implications be because we have learned that we must move from the paranoid-schizoid to the depressive. Can you explain a little about that?

Response 2

Yes, well I think that Dr. Scharff should take another look. Perhaps he has not gone deep enough. But yes, I am very moved that you are moved. It makes me feel like crying that some bit of what I am trying to communicate has actually touched somebody. In the epilogue of *The Electrified Tightrope* I talk about child analysts and grown up analysts, and child patients and grown up patients. I don't mean children literally. I mean analysts who are more childlike and analysts who are more adult and grown up, and patients who are more childlike and patients who are more adult and grown up and perhaps more buttoned up. Sometimes a child patient will get matched up with a grown up analyst and it might not work out as well as it could. What I felt and still feel now is that you can't and ought not try to turn someone into someone who he isn't. There is a who, a who you are, your psychic DNA. Not the environment, not the conditioning, but the naked, naked self—you. And if you are a child, you are going to remain a child forever. Yesterday Jae took us to the king's palace and he had made a lovely luncheon appointment at a great dumpling place. But just as we were beginning to leave to go to lunch they had the changing of the guards' ceremony. And myself particularly and my wife and my son wanted to see it. It was magnificent. I am a musician so I loved the music with the big trumpets with the conch shells with the little trumpets with the drums. Marvelous! And Jae kept grabbing me by the elbow. You have to go to lunch; you have to go to lunch. I have an appointment. And I didn't know what to do because I kept going back and watching the parade. And finally I think I said, "Jae! I'm I child! I want to see this." And then it was OK. And we did get to the dumpling restaurant and we had a good lunch. You have to stay with the real.

Over the course of my lifetime, I'm in my seventies, I've become a better child, a fuller child, not a more mature child—I'm pretty bad—but I've become a better version of myself. More of me has had a chance to enter the field of life. Now if I had been an adult self, I would hope over the course of my life to become a better adult. I don't expect to turn an adult into a child or a child into an adult, but I do hope to create conditions for the person to blossom as the kind of person they really are and about that there aren't judgments.

Question 3

I want to ask a question related to biblical teaching. Actually it is so much internalized this denial of self. So how do we integrate object relations and what do you suggest we do to remain real to ourselves and to be healthy and also follow the doctrine to not be self-seeking.

Response 3

Even the child struggles with the pain of what it means to be a person. Even if one doesn't quite know what one is struggling with, or what kind of person one is or can become, still one struggles. Your question I think is very important because so often spirituality forces the matter too quickly, forces one into this or that too quickly. Religion's had a horrible history of putting people in hell, putting people in heaven. Splitting that makes these divisions even more painful. If I were a pastoral counselor my spiritual advice would be, don't rush, don't rush. If there is a loved one in trouble and there's a conflict between your selfishness and putting the other first, well if the situation requires putting the other first, then you will do that. You'll feel it. You'll know you have to do it. And there will be other situations that don't require that in which you say, "Well this time I'm putting myself first and it's not a big deal." But that's not the point. The point that is relevant and that I'm trying to convey is the Christian teaching: forgive them father they don't know what they are doing. They don't know. Forgive them. They don't know. They think they know. They act like they know. They talk like they know. But dear God we don't know. And that is the teaching, the main teaching, the central teaching and things flow, things grow. You don't have to force it so much.

What I'm about to say now may not be relevant to the question. I'm going off to something that bothers me. Bush, the president of my country, who may never have been fairly elected, seems to be an example of someone God spoke to. God told him "Invade Iraq." Corporations also told him "Invade Iraq." The idea of waiting, of waiting and seeing what unfolds wasn't part of the public discourse, didn't occur as a real possibility. Waiting means you'll seem weak; you'll look like you don't know what you are doing. Better to kill and be a bully and act strong than say, "I don't know, I'm waiting a while."

There is much external pressure to know or to act like one knows. And there is a dim quiet internal invitation not to know. Let God do the work. Let Tao do the work. Let something unknown come help you out. Leave room for the deeper processes that you don't have access to at this time. Trying too hard to go this way or that way stops or prevents a deeper contact, a deeper access from having more input. And the way Bush acted with Iraq could have been for corporate motives or for religious motives, but not religion in our sense. That same pressure we see outside in politics happens inside us. The bully, the bully self, the tyrant saying to do it this way. This is the way it's got to be done. You're weak or cowardly if you just wait or surrender or take your time or listen, listen, listen. I love the big ears of the Buddha that I see as I go around. And I think that's what psychoanalysis ought to use as its logo. Like a new way of listening, a new way of hearing oneself.

Question 4

You said that we must stay with our essence. Personally I have been searching and get lost trying to find my essence. Dr. Eigen if you could share what you are doing to find your essence it would be of great help to me. I have several questions but I will start with this one.

Response 4

Don't use me as a model. If essence is confusing, being nothing is good too. There is a Jewish joke I don't remember altogether but it has to do with someone feeling bad about himself and goes around saying "I'm a nothing, I'm a nothing," And his friend says, "Look who's calling himself a nothing." It's a kind of grandiose statement, quite an achievement. I guess there are lots of kinds of nothings.

But more seriously, if one is feeling nothing then that is what one needs to taste, one needs to taste it, not be defensive about it. Be with it, be with that nothing. That nothing needs you and perhaps you need it. And if my remark about essence is persecutory to you, if it bothers you, forget about it, chuck it. It's probably just a stupid thing that I said at the spur of the moment.

Question 5

Listening to your talk Dr. Eigen, it is clear that we humans try everything to avoid pain but that it is inevitable. I too realized that I have tried to avoid pain and lost many things in the process and this saddened me greatly today. Thank you for the insight. When I meet patients they dump all sorts of things on me and among them I feel immense pain and despair and as a therapist I am suddenly confused at how I will contend with these things. I would appreciate if you could help me with this.

Response 5

We would all like that help. And we all need that help. Thank you. Tomorrow we will be talking about a scream that's inside. This scream never goes away, it's there all one's life. Just because one is a baby and stops screaming, it doesn't mean that the scream goes away inside. There is a scream that goes on all life long no matter who we are or what we do. Some of us manifest that scream by creating wars. Some of us withdraw from it or hide from it. Some of us beat up anyone that comes near us. Or we are screaming at ourselves and some of us commit suicide when the scream reaches too unbearable a point. But the scream goes on whether we are alive or whether we are dead. We can't stop that scream. That scream has to be experienced. It has to be tasted and one has to learn to be with that scream in some way. Perhaps not all out fully, totally. That may not be possible or even desirable but in doses, doses you can work with. Not in doses that you cannot tolerate, but in doses that you can begin to work with, to process the scream that never goes away. Many years ago when I wrote a book called *Psychic Deadness*, I talked about a wound that never heals and I talked about a fire that never goes out. A good fire, a creative fire, not the bad fire. The wound that never heals meets the fire that never goes out. It's a lifelong process of recovery. Not simply covering oneself up again or becoming a full person that one isn't, a phony full person. But one gets more of an ability, a tiny bit more of an ability to say "Ah that scream, that's me. That's my life. My life is a scream in disguise." It's not only that, but it's also that. Oh what to do with patients. Be with the pain.

There are lots of ways of being with pain without trying to alter it. I wouldn't say necessarily honour it, but give the patient room to have it because everyone is trying to make it go away. Everyone is trying to say "Oh it's not really that bad, or it's not really there, or it shouldn't be there, do this, do that, exercise more, take more medicine. I don't know what. But to just let the pain be, not expecting anything, not putting pressure on it. We put so much pressure on ourselves in so many ways. It's a difference inside you when you are sitting with someone's pain and you stop expecting yourself to ease the pain in the person. I can't explain it. It's taking pressure off yourself, cultural pressure.

Here is a little example. It is about a man I wrote about in *Toxic Nourishment* and *Damaged Bonds*. I called him Milton. He is a man who has been in pain all his life, pain that won't go away. I don't know whether it will ever go away or not. I have no idea and he doesn't either. It is awful. He would commit suicide if not for what I'm not sure—maybe his children, maybe something more, a kind of deep dedication to the truth of life, his truth. He is devoted to inner truthfulness. We have been together many years, and he was in therapy many more years with people before me. He is trying to make contact—with himself, with life. He is committed to his search. To be present in his search yet not able to be present in life—to be present at all is a plus. For some, being present to one's non-presence may be better than not being there and not knowing it. For Milton, it's a must.

A few weeks ago he said, "I feel my father killed me or some part of me." And I said I absolutely believe you. And he weeps. After a long silence he says, "When I heard your words I felt an entity leave me." That's the little vignette. He's not cured, I'm not cured. I'm in pain, he's in pain. I'm broken, he's broken. But this moment, this one little moment when he felt, actually felt, took many years to find. These weren't wasted years. They could look wasted. Some therapists wouldn't have been able to stand it. But these years weren't wasted because a moment arrived in which he felt my belief in his pain. For an instant he believed that I actually believed he was in pain and that this pain could be permanent. He heard me and for a moment felt my affirmation of the truth of his feeling. A feeling that came through was "Yes I absolutely, absolutely believe you." And he said, "When I heard you, when I heard your words I felt an entity leave me." In the United States an entity is like a devil, a possessed state. Now, I know that if one entity leaves there are probably a million more. But it was a precious moment that took years to happen. No insurance company would pay for this moment. But it is an eternal moment. A moment that makes a difference to the universe forever. And some of you may be feeling ripples of it today.

CHAPTER TWO

Day 2

Winnicott and Bion

Morning session: Screaming and singing: The dream scream

I'm glad some people came back. Any questions or thoughts or things you thought about overnight? We can start out with those, anything more from yesterday? Everything!

Question 1

You said yesterday that 'We have to stay real.' What state is this 'real' and is it what Winnicott calls the true self? I would like to know about this 'real.'

Response 1

You're thinking too hard. We don't know. We can't answer it in discursive terms. We will never know. It is beyond our capabilities. It's just a way of speaking, of touching what we imagine to be a continuum. Winnicott's false self, true self is really a continuum, a fusion, a mixture. It's not a dichotomy. It's not as dichotomous as he makes it. It's all mixed up. It's indistinguishable. We can't tell one from the other a lot of the time. Sometimes we think we can. But we often turn out to be wrong. What we thought was true turns out to be an illusion, what we thought was false turns out to be the best thing in us. But we try, we try to be true. We try to be real. But everything here is real, we are all real. Everything is real, a lie is real. I wish I had brought with me a little quote from Winnicott. He says, something like the mature person is one who can compromise, one who can lie and one who can be flexible and not too hard on oneself for one's failings. The psychotic is inflexible, the psychotic can't lie. The psychotic can't compromise. It's interesting too that Winnicott remarked about Van Gogh, too much true self.

Yesterday some people asked about giving up this or giving up that. My aim is not to make dualities worse, not to make the war between tendencies stronger, not to increase the bifurcations, but to broaden the psychic field to make room for all tendencies, to make room for a psychic democracy where all our tendencies, all our capacities have a voice, all have input, all have the potential to give something to life. Every bit of us has the potential to give something to life. It's a matter of getting a context for it, a broadening the field, broadening the playground, the inner and outer playground, the playground of the self. If you don't like the word self substitute whatever works for you. To broaden the playground of the psyche, not to increase the wars. The wars have been around for a long time.

The Greeks heard the music of the spheres, heard the cosmic music, they wrote about the cosmic music. But they also wrote about the war between all elements, that nature was made up of a war between all elements. That appealed to Freud. Not the music of the spheres. Maybe Freud wasn't listening to the cosmic music or maybe he was. But what appealed to him was the war, the conflict, that things grow through conflict. As Mao Tsae Tung said, conflict produces change. Marion Milner liked Mao Tsae Tung's idea of conflict producing change. But in her terms the idea of conflict producing change was a part of a larger psychic field in which the relationship between our tendencies, between our capacities keeps changing. Sometimes they are in conflict, sometimes they are antagonist, sometimes they are co-nourishing, mutually dependent, sometimes they fuse. Mixtures of tendencies, capacities, voices keep on changing.

DAY 2   23

And what do we hear, psychoanalysts? We hear the music of the psyche. We hear the psyche's music. And we know about psychic struggle. Psychic struggle is part of our psychic field, conflict a basic psychic ingredient. We also know that there is a beatific core, some kind of beatific element too, a bliss at the center of the storm. But there is a real storm and there is a real bliss somewhere in the center of it holding it all together too.

Anyone else want to try to get me to make a response to something? Don't give up on me. Sometimes it takes ten tries to make something happen.

Question 2

It is good to see you again. Listening to you today, I had the thought that psychoanalysis is not only the most thorough way to analyze a human being but also can free us in the fullest way. On the other hand, not on a micro-level but for example in the Iraq invasion, family is destroyed and the child will grow up with revenge and rage in their heart. Organizations and nations ruin lives. In other words, traditionally in psychoanalysis trauma was inflicted by significant others but in times such as ours where the system or nation or world is inflicting overwhelming trauma, what does psychoanalysis tell us and what does it have to contribute?

Response 2

Very important issue. How far can we go with it now, I don't know. I have a book on the Internet called *Age of Psychopathy* (2006). And it's about what you are talking about. We are living in a psychopathic age. Psychopathy as a term is not used anymore in the United States. It involves not having a conscience, not caring what happens to other people as long as you are boss, as long as you get your way, as long as you are the winner, as long as you are on top of the economic chain, the power chain. Not caring what you have to do to others in order to be on top. It's an economic age, an economically driven age. Still, we see every now and then something human. In the middle of Seoul there is water, a little river, a brook that flows through the city and makes people happy. That's something human. My wife and I were impressed that someone did something so smart for a city. Some architect or politician or combination were smart enough to make something that people can enjoy in the middle of the city, people with their feet in the water, music in the night. A very different model of human life than the predator-prey model, which seems to rule most of politics. We're always delighted by human miracles, little openings of another model, another way of doing something where nourishment and caring for people is the model rather than the economic power, predator-prey model. In my recent books, *Age of Psychopathy* and *Feeling Matters* (2006) I talk about just what you are saying. The rape of the people, the trauma inflicted by the system, by the establishment and wars of subsystems.

It's even worse than you say, at least as I understand it. In my country there is corporate control of the media, of the news on TV. So people get to see what passes the censorship. It's a George Orwell kind of world in which the government serves corporate power and the media serves the government. It's quite a horrifying state to be in at this point. There are intriguing things about this system. When I was a young boy growing up corporations tried to make a profit. They tried to be profitable and they had systems to help their workers. They had support for their workers and it was kind of mutually fruitful. There was antagonism, strikes, the workers wanted more so they went on strike and tried to get a little more. But I don't know what to call it. It was more honest than it is today somewhat. Now you don't have to make a profit to win. Your business can lose. Your government can fail. Your war can be a disaster. You can have a war that loses. But the people running the corporations make money on it. They make money on a business that loses. They make money on a war that fails, a war that is a disaster. The tie between winning and ethics and the profit motive is already on the way to extinction. It's just a toy in a bigger game. You can lose to win now. You don't have to win to win. So the situation is even worse that you are depicting.

The Zen teacher that I saw a few days ago asked the same question and he didn't really have an answer either. Neither he, neither psychoanalysis nor Buddhism at this point has an answer. His tactic, his strategy at the moment seems to be environmental activity. He seems to feel there is an opening, a place that he can exert pressure, put an effort in that can bear some kind of fruit that can get in under the radar system. We'll see. Certainly there are more environmental protests going on in the United States now and even some of the Christian fundamentalists are beginning to become concerned about the environment. That's new in the United States. Previously they sided with the corporations and big money. Now some of them are beginning to think Jesus may not have been a supply side economist. Maybe Jesus had a different perception of the distribution of goods.

A theme in *Feeling Matters* is the sense of helplessness that people feel. In the United States for the last seven years there has been an increased sense of helplessness: 'What can one do in face of the great machine that seems to be trampling over everybody?' Bush didn't win an election. The Supreme Court of the land falsified itself and gave him the election. When you have models of thievery at the very highest places, criminality at the very highest places in government, the very highest defender of the law the Supreme Court of the land engaging in criminal decisions—what kind of model is that for the society? What kind of model is that for the average person? It promotes psychopathy all through the social fabric. It promotes psychopathy in psychoanalysis as well. It makes for a psychopathic atmosphere. The majority of the public does not support the Bush regime and its machinations.

There is a special ingredient that politicians have always used but the Bush group has used immensely. One of the mechanisms they use to keep the population down is the psychopathic manipulation of psychotic anxieties. They keep stirring catastrophic fears, psychotic anxieties, annihilation anxieties and manipulate these anxieties in order to maintain power. It works for 40% of the population and the other 60% of the population are like Lilliputians hitting a great giant. It's like being in a soundproof room where you can't hear your own voice or have an effect on the system because the system is at the moment in ascension.

In the United States many psychoanalysts are engaging in some form of political action. We don't know now what is going to happen. It's not the first time in human history that things have looked grim. It's rather the case in human history that it's rare that it is otherwise. So one goes on with one's life the best one can of course. Life is life. But it is not impossible to exert some pressure on the system in different ways. There are a lot of action groups in the States that are trying to do this. I don't know the situation here. I hope you have a better situation. But I have a hunch that what is happening in the States is eventually, if not already, going to be fairly worldwide. Because the corporate lust for power is worldwide.

In *Feeling Matters* I write about the reciprocal influence of society and the family and the individual. For example, a case of child abuse. In one case, a patient who was abused as a child reacted to the 2000 election as if it were a kind of political abuse. Her background of child abuse and the reality of political abuse fused and empowered each other and led to growth on her part because she was able to see the reality of political abuse because of working on her own early familial abuse. The political abuse of the nation became part of the psychoanalysis, part of a freeing growth.

In our work you go back and forth between family trauma and economic social trauma. It is all part of one cloth, one fabric. It is us. It is the reality that people have created. We have created this. We do this. And we don't know what to do with what we create. We create good things and we create monsters. And we don't know how to use what we created. It is very much unsolved, very much in progress.

Well, I've been told by a higher power to start what I was going to do so we'll do that. But one more note. I never thought that I would write so much about politics and psychoanalysis as I've done in the past several years. That's not my vocation. If it's not your vocation to be a political activist you shouldn't do it. If your vocation is to just live your own particular life, be a psychoanalyst, do the normal things that a human being does in every day life, then that's what you do. You have to pursue your calling, your vocation, what's right for you. Being a political activist isn't really right for me. I do some but it's not really right for me. I write about it more than I do it. My wife does it more than I do. I can't believe that I wrote so much about politics in the past several years. But I've never been so traumatized by the political machinations that occurred. I can't tell you what a traumatic shock it's been, the way this group has taken over power in the country. It's astonishing. Maybe I'm naïve. I didn't think I had many illusions about what politicians do but this was stunning. I wouldn't say it woke me up. But I had to write in response to the criminal abuse of the country, the criminal abuse of life. There is a war between a nourishing model of life and a predator-prey model of life.

OK now we'll scream.

Yesterday we talked about annihilation. Annihilation is not a terminal stop; it is not a static state. It goes on and on and on. It's electrifying.

I don't have the words for it. It's like being in an electric chair with the current continuously on, or being suffocated but you never die. You keep getting more and more suffocated. I don't know if they use insulin shock anymore for psychosis. It's not as terrible as some of the things that have been used for psychosis. But one thing that happens in insulin shock for many people, is that they wake up during the coma. You're put in a coma, the coma varies, and you come in and out of consciousness. You fade into consciousness, go out of consciousness. When you come into consciousness in insulin shock and begin going out of consciousness, you feel like you are dying. You scream. When I heard patients in this state I felt that this is partly what babies must feel, in their own way, when they go in and out of consciousness. Screaming and screaming and then the scream fades away.

When I was a young man I tried different therapies. Some of them involved screaming, like primal scream therapy. We screamed and screamed. And it did me good. You feel your body tissues, your body aliveness. I used to imagine in New York City there should be little boxes on the street like little phone booths. They would be scream booths. People could just go into them when they needed to and scream. There would be a screaming place.

Winnicott's (1992, pp. 115–118; Eigen, 2002, pp. 151–155) approach is different and very profound. It's not the patient screaming, it is the patient hearing and feeling and coming in contact with the scream within. It is not extroverted. It is not so American extroverted. It is more British schizoid-introverted, feeling the scream within. The two approaches are good. All genuine approaches are good. But Winnicott adds something that is very delicate, very important.

Before getting deeper into Winnicott's scream, I want to add one more note on annihilation and annihilation anxiety. Winnicott pictures a situation in which the baby is left by the mother. The baby is left by the mother for X amount of time. Mother comes back, nurses the baby, touches the baby, smiles at the baby. The baby comes alive. And life goes on. There is a mild experience of fading out and coming back. One of the theories in insulin shock coma was that you die out and come back and see the world in a different way. Russian doctors went further, putting individuals to sleep for six months, sleep therapy. They would put them out of commission for six months, then wake them up again, hoping they would undercut the psychosis and see life in a new way.

In my book, *Coming Through the Whirlwind* (1992) I try to communicate a kind of rebirth model. Going out, coming back, dying out, coming back, and how complicated this is. Sometimes you die out and come back the wrong way. It's not easy to die out and come back in a fruitful way. Sometimes you die out and come back like a monster. A lot of factors go into this. This book tries to show some of the processes involved. For example, there's Winnicott's baby dying out for time X, mother comes and baby revives. Then there is dying out for time X plus Y, longer. Mother comes back and baby revives again, comes back into life. Still OK. One gets practice in sustaining discontinuity, coming back, dying out, coming back. It becomes part of one's rhythm. And then he writes about mother leaving and baby dying out X plus Y plus Z time. Mother comes back but baby does not simply come alive as before. In the Z dimension, baby undergoes a change, a permanent alteration, damage. Something tight, angry, something wrong, something withdrawn. Spontaneous recovery doesn't happen. In therapy with certain people more than others, it's the Z dimension we focus on, a dying out we don't return from, that we live around, develop paranoia around, or anger around, or withdraw around. We are not worried about X or X plus Y—they take care of themselves. We worry more about the Z dimension. In certain cases, it is the Z dimensions we need to live our way into and address.

In the chapter "Screaming" in my book, *Rage,* I portray screams in my life and in Bion's and Winnicott's work. I wrote the book a little before the World Trade Center bombing and added a section on the bombing afterwards. From what I wrote in the book, you could see the bombing was predictable. It was part of the temper of the times, the rage of the times. Explosions everywhere. In our country, in our computer age, people would kill each other over a parking space. Road rage, computer rage, economic rage, class and race rage, fundamentalist rage. Rage was proliferating. I suspect part of the rage comes from the Z dimension.

Winnicott and Bion both write about a different kind of connection between dream and reality. They say something that I think involves a step in evolution in our thinking about ourselves. They overlap in saying that dreaming makes things real. Things entering us have to enter us partly through our dream work in order for them to become real, to become part of us, a living part of our existence.

A paradoxical way of thinking: dreaming makes life real, makes reality real. It is not a simple thought. There's a lot of subtlety here. Both Bion and Winnicott elaborate it in special ways throughout their work.

The scream that most interests Winnicott is a psychic scream, a scream within. Winnicott writes of a dream scream, a patient dreaming of screaming. Apparently infants can dream with their eyes open and dreaming may be part of screaming. A baby's screaming may be similar to dreaming. Even after external screaming fades, a dream scream continues. As time goes on, we make contact with our screaming beings through dreaming. We need to dream our scream for it to become real and we need to experience our dream as part of the realizing process. Screaming partly tries to scream screaming away. It is a communication that, at the same time, conveys and tries to blot out experience. We can scream so much we no longer feel the feeling, yet screaming was precipitated by feeling. Dreams preserve the need to scream and become a mode of contact with ourselves. As Bion and Winnicott suggest, inner and outer events have to enter dream work to become part of our insides. Our need to scream also undergoes a dream journey.

For Bion, the question of how something comes in, letting things in, how they become part of us, is a problem. It's as if he says, "We can't let too much in. We don't let too much in. We don't let enough in." At the same time even a little may seem like too much. Yet you have to let in, in order to love. You have to let in, in order to for your heart to embrace somebody. But how to let in? What if the capacity to let in, to let something become part of you has become damaged? We produce, we push out, we make things. We make economic toys, we make products, we make mental products, we make emotional products, we make material products. And we can't assimilate the products of our thoughts, we can't keep up with them. We can't assimilate what we are producing. We produce thoughts and feelings faster than we can take in, faster than we can take them in and digest them.

Dreamwork for Winnicott and Bion is one way, an important way, perhaps a crucial way, of taking things in and beginning to work on them, beginning to digest experience rather than just have experience, experience, experience. It's a way to begin to get something out of the experience, to use the experience, to digest the experience.

Dreamwork is part of our psychic digestive system. Things become real for us by dreaming them, become emotionally important by dreaming. In the case of Winnicott's patient I want to talk about today, the scream became real by dreaming about it. She might have been in pain, might have been screaming all her life inside, but she hadn't made contact with her scream in a way she could use. She hadn't made contact with her scream in a way she could take in, take herself in, make contact with herself, be with herself. It was through a dream that the scream became real for her.

This patient had skin eruptions, eczema, pimples. Winnicott relates skin eruptions and breathing problems to a psychotic area of the psyche. The case I am speaking of comes from "Additional Notes on Psycho-Somatic Disorder," in Winnicott's *Psychoanalytic Explorations*. In general, he tends to relate psychosomatic problems to a dissociated psychotic sector of the psyche. The patient he describes has skin eruptions and strained body states, hyper vigilant tension. She became aware of a screaming feeling, a need to scream. I don't know how often the need to scream is recognized as one of the human needs, but Winnicott recognizes a need to scream.

The scream this patient contacted in her body tension was a failed scream, an aborted scream, a stillborn scream, a vanishing scream. She said it was a scream that she was always not experiencing. Winnicott called it the great non-event of every session. The vanishing scream, the stillborn scream. The failed scream was the great non-event of every session, the thing that didn't happen. Winnicott felt the scream that she was looking for was 'The last scream just before hope was abandoned.' He felt the scream she was looking for was the last scream just before hope was lost, before all hope disappeared. With the disappearance of the scream came the disappearance of hope. What is important is not simply screaming, but a loss of a capacity, a loss of an ability—an inability to scream. A little like the helplessness felt in America over the current traumatic regime. It's almost as if the ability to effect things has been lost. Winnicott emphasizes nuances of lost screams.

The capacity to scream can't be taken for granted. Winnicott depicts what I called the Z situation, in which a mother does not respond to a baby's cry until the baby feels it is no use, and screaming fails its purpose. Communication at the level of screaming is jeopardized. As you know screaming is a communication and if there is no response, if it's a voice, a scream, crying in the wilderness, that form of communication gets jeopardized, undergoes deformation. If the earliest processes of communication undergo deformation, we are dealing with deformation of a personality before processes like splitting occur. Splitting doesn't apply here. It's too structured, it's too me-you, this-that. We are talking here about a different nuance, a different capacity. So if the scream isn't responded to, it begins to be lost, it begins not to be a scream.

The scream, if it still goes on, is inaudible, not hearable. Some people feel invisible, some people feel inaudible, they can't be heard and they can't hear themselves. In therapy, the lost scream has a chance of surfacing. It surfaces because it has a partner, someone who hears it. In fact, the therapist may hear the scream as soon as the patient walks into the office. One may not say anything about it for years. One may not have an opportunity for it to make sense for a long time. But it is not unusual to feel the scream in the patient, the inaudible scream. It is not unusual for it to be transmitted immediately: as soon as you see the person you see a scream, a scream that can't be felt, an unknown scream.

It's not unusual for a person to be a walking scream at various degrees of knowability and unknowability. A therapist knows about soul screams. Winnicott speaks of a scream linking psyche and soma. Insofar as the scream is lost, a certain link between psyche and soma is lost. Winnicottt says that a positive function of crying, screaming, yelling, angry protest, can be an immense strengthening of the psycho-somatic relationship. That's what I experienced when I was young and screaming in scream therapy. It took me many more years to catch up with the inside scream. There is an immense strengthening of the psychosomatic relationship, interrelationship, when one recovers the dream scream. The dream scream adds to the psychosomatic flow. There is less need to artificially keep oneself in life. A theme in Winnicott's work is how we force ourselves to be in life, to keep in life. A forcing that revs life up at life's expense.

One woman Winnicott describes tried to keep herself in life in order to keep her mother in life. If she let herself drop out of life for a moment, she feared her mother would collapse or die psychologically. She had to be turned on in order to make her mother feel alive. She had to be her mother's transitional object. She did not have a chance not to be. It takes quite some effort to force oneself to always be, to act alive, smile or otherwise be her mother's life force. The mother depended on her child's vital emotional aliveness for reassurance. Winnicott's patient could never just not be. She couldn't be dead. Her mother couldn't take it. So Winnicott's patient couldn't just be. She had to keep reviving herself and be and be and be more in order to support her mother's need for her never to drop out of being.

It's important for us to give each other room not to be. Otherwise our being will be forced. There is a Taoist text that talks about a need to be dead in life. Being too much in life one can lose oneself. One can become dead to oneself by trying to be too alive. Winnicott is sensitive to forcing oneself to be alive, instead of just going with the rhythm of being alive, being less alive, being out of it, not being there, coming back, back and forth.

I remember in my twenties working with autistic children. One day a lovely autistic girl climbs in a baby carriage and lies on her back. She has her hands up above her head and is totally open. It's like she is in heaven for a moment. Not having to rush around, not being active, not having to be restless. A totally relaxed moment, something Winnicott aims for in certain parts of his therapy. Just to let go, let go of being. Just to float, not be there, be there, it doesn't matter anymore. Her therapist comes along, a positive, good willed young woman, a very active person. She sees her little girl patient lying in the baby carriage and goes over to the girl and playfully pokes her chest with her finger, saying "Poop, poop, poop." She tries to tickle her or poke her to get a response. It's like throwing a rock into the water. And then you see the girl in a state of alarm. Her peace is broken, a shock. I was astonished and felt the shock waves, the ripples. I can feel them now, more than fifty years later. That moment is like a model of what we shouldn't do to each other. It's like a model of what we shouldn't do to each other's peace. It's something for therapists to think twice about, breaking into a peaceful experience of the patient because they have something else in mind, or they don't think the patient is doing it right. Perhaps the mother who does this needs entertainment, or needs aliveness, or a different kind of aliveness. So this very alive young therapist was too alive in an active way at that moment for her patient, who was alive in a very different way. The child was alive in a way that I recognized in some of the Korean landscape paintings I saw the other day, a different kind of aliveness. It's not unusual to have a problem mismatching active and passive. It is a problem I've thought about for years. Certain good meaning, active people may not have a passive side, may be afraid of their passive side. The reverse also holds. Some may be more at peace with passivity and afraid of activity. It can go either way. Subtle matches and mismatches play an important role in the background of how we grow and feel.

I remember looking at my children, each of my two sons very different from the moment of birth. One seemed at harmony with everything and one looked fierce. The one who was at harmony with everything could simply get into the same pose, the same state and stay there. He would gaze and it would be like a gaze into an infinite horizon. It could be in heaven, it could be nowhere. I learned a lot by watching him and feeling what it must be like to be in that state. That is a state to honour, and it's a thread that runs through life. When I was a young man I had the honour to see both D. T. Suzuki one year and a few years later, Martin Buber—two great spiritual seekers (Eigen, 1998). I remember Suzuki talking about the seven levels of love. In the question period he said something that was for me an instantaneous awakening. It played a role in my life ever since. It was like a jolt, a good jolt. Someone in the audience asked a question that had something to do with activity, passivity. There is a tendency to overvalue the former and undervalue the latter in our culture. This bias is part of psychoanalytic theory (e.g., libido is defined as active, a parallel to Aristotle's God as active reason). For years in psychoanalysis, passivity was associated with fear, or an inferior position, or something inert, even dead. If one digs a little more, one sees that passivity is associated with trauma, fear of castration or annihilation, fear of passively being traumatized. There are those who fear they will be injured if they are passive and those who fear they will be injured if they are active. Even in Buddhist literature and talks I attended, there was care to point out that what seemed like passive in meditation was alive and alert, not inert. They were concerned that passivity would be devalued so they had to make sure people understood that passivity wasn't really passive. When Suzuki was asked this question he simply said (he was in his nineties at that time) "Passivity, passivity! What's wrong with passivity?" He said that his favourite things in America are passive pleasures—going to the movies, just watching the screen, being taken here and there on airplanes. And it was like, yes passivity! An unembarrassed affirmation of passivity. Passivity, in part, is devalued now because it is not adaptive to our active society. One can't honor the passive side of one's baby self. One has to be an active baby.

It's easy to value one capacity over another, to split bits of our make-up and say this is good, that is bad, to side with one over another. Not that the world of splitting is wrong; the language of splitting has its uses. But it may not do justice to early formations, atmospheric conditions in which self or personality begin to form, atmospheric formation of the self, the taste and smell of one's life. Freud writes that tendencies that seem separate in later life may be indistinguishable at their origins. Winnicott takes us past splitting when he touches the response of the environment, the response of the other as part of the psychic air one breathes, mixtures of toxins and nourishment. It's the atmosphere that supports our life and deforms our life as we are beginning to form, as we are beginning to come into life. In this regard, the therapy atmosphere may be more important than any particular thing the analyst says or does, and everything we do or say is important in some way. What's more important is the psychic atmosphere, the conditions that are being set for a transmission that can take many years and can change the balance of a person's life.

Winnicott believes his patient's ability to dream the scream, the scream she lost, became possible as the result of her analysis in which hope about dreaming returned, enabling contact with healthier elements of her life. This is a strong statement. One thing in reading Winnicott is that he writes so gently you don't realize how strongly he is speaking. What he says is very powerful, very rigorous, very strong. But you can miss it because his words melt like butter. I don't know what he sounds like in Korean. But in English, his words are very gentle and you can miss the impact of how profound he is.

In English, reading Winnicott is like experiencing a good mother. A mother that sees, not a blind mother. A mother that sees and feels. There is a connection between seeing and feeling. In English, reading Melanie Klein is like a war. It is violent. And they are both important and they are both us.

For Winnicott dreaming plays an important role in psychic aliveness. Therapy plays an important role in supporting dreaming. We may be in process of trying to develop more of a language for such underpinnings. In America one may say, 'It is only a dream.' 'It was just a nightmare.' Yet for Bion, there are ways psychic work begins and is challenged by nightmares. A therapist who values psychic reality may feel, "Ah, therapy is starting, he had a nightmare." His psyche is now telling the truth. It's showing what it's like to be alive for this person, in this case catastrophic aliveness. I remember a therapy experience I had years ago with Fritz Perls, who developed what he called gestalt therapy. He would have us tell our dreams and then be all the things in the dream. If a table appeared in the dream, we would be the table. We would speak from the "perspective" of all the parts of the dream, give them voice. And he would make us say, before we said anything else, before we even told the dream, "This dream is my existence."

So when we devalue a dream, when it's 'only a dream', we devalue the psyche. Our culture devalues the psyche unless it can make a profit from it. The psyche is something to manipulate, to use, to make a movie, to sell a book, start a war, exploit, make money. There is not much room for the psyche for its own sake. There is not much of a place for it. Artists are trying and some psychoanalysts are trying. Some of us are trying this very moment.

The intensity and duration in which Winnicott's patient had to bear the sense of loss of an absent or missing scream, paved a way for a deeper appreciation for the feeling of screaming when it actually began to appear. What is most important for Winnicott is not the scream. The scream too easily becomes an object that doesn't matter, a kind of psychic commodity. What is important is the feeling of the scream that the dream tries to preserve. Just like when the psychotic goes under during insulin shock treatment. There is feeling there, a horrible feeling of course, but it's like the dream scream. It's real. In a sense there is a way in which there is no difference between nightmares and dreams, and nightmares and reality. What is happening to the Iraqi population, that's a real nightmare. And it fits in with and has resonance with our own internal states.

Although there are practical differences, there is a way in which the self and the world are all one fabric. One can't solve political problems and leave the psyche out, just as we have to think of society's impingement on the psyche. Problems aren't going to be solved without work on a psychic level as well. We need to work on both psychic and social levels. It's not one or the other. They are both in the equation. They are both part of the same fabric.

Now, feeling the scream. It's the same problem that exercises Bion. How can we dream something into a feeling state, make it real for us, make it a felt reality, make it something we can taste, smell, breathe, and be part of our lives and not simply deny and hallucinate away. Winnicott opens us to a felt scream, not just a scream, a feeling scream. He says the dream scream opens the possibility of being connected to the life of feeling. This is a strong statement, which I may not be saying right. The dream scream opens the possibility of feeling and connects waking and sleeping. So waking and sleeping work together in their different forms of being, different forms of consciousness or unconsciousness. And Winnicott proposes that feeling connects them.

Bion, too, is concerned with the link between waking and sleeping. He is especially concerned about Freud's statement that the job of psychoanalysis is to make the unconscious conscious. Bion felt that for our time, it is more important to learn how to make the conscious unconscious. To take in, to let life be part of one. To take in the world, take in the other, take in one's own thoughts, take in one's own contact with one's being. How to become real to oneself in some way or how to link up with oneself in some way. The word self is just a notation. So in this case, in the dream scream, the scream itself, the screaming has lots of colors. It's a spectrum. Screaming is like a prism. It has lots of parts to it. If you listen to a scream, feel a scream, let it permeate you, you'll see it made up of lots of filaments, lots of colours on the emotional spectrum. Not one thing. Nothing in the psyche is one thing. It's lots of filaments, lots of combinations of colors. And in the scream, two of the many colours in the emotional spectrum involve something like outrage and anguish. It's almost as if one is feeling distress about something that shouldn't be there. It's like an ethics. In a way the scream has an ethics in it: 'This shouldn't be happening. Something is wrong.' And there is an outrage and anguish about it. And therapy offers the possibility of letting this sense of outrage and anguish turn into communicative links with oneself and with others.

I want to add something many of you may already have heard. A little anecdote concerning a dream by Clare Winnicott after Winnicott's death. Clare Winnicott somehow didn't fully believe that he was dead. She was almost living as if he was with her, or was going to be with her, or soon to appear, or to come back from the vacation that he was taking and probably forget what it was he was supposed to bring her. In his lifetime, whenever she sent him out for something, he'd forget it. Once she fell down and hurt herself and she needed a bandage. She sent him out to the drugstore to get a bandage and he came back with a book and forgot the bandage. So he seemed not to remember too well what her needs were in certain ways. He would get absorbed in something else and forget about it. So she almost expected him to absentmindedly walk through the door with whatever it was he'd forgotten. And then she had a dream in which D.W. appeared in the dream and said, "You know Clare, I'm dead." And then she got it. It became part of her. And then it became real, really real.

* * *

Afternoon session: A half filled cup

Now let's try a little taste of Bion. In the time period we have which seems a lot but which is really very, very little we're lucky if we are able to create a tiny sample of all this, but a fair sample, a good sample. If we can create a good sample, it is better than saying a lot of things that don't add up to anything. Our entire three day seminar is just a sample, a little dip into certain aspects of psychic reality through the lenses, through the eyes of Klein, Winnicott, Bion and of course Eigen. I'm the filter for all three of them today and so are you. If you want to look more into what we are doing, you can find writings on Klein in *The Psychotic Core*, *Psychic Deadness*, and *Feeling Matters*. I wrote about screaming in *Rage*. Writings on the structure of Bion's clinical vignettes are in *Damaged Bonds*, *The Sensitive Self*, and *The Psychoanalytic Mystic*. The one I draw on most today is from *The Sensitive Self*.

Jae [Jae hoon Lee, founder of the Object Relations Institute in Seoul] asked me what book of mine he should translate if he is going to undertake that task. And I suggested for the group here a book called *Toxic Nourishment*. It is very accessible. It is very deep. It has chapters on suicide, on abortion, on working in deep areas with the self. Much discussion about current day concerns and much discussion about the deep psyche in its psychotic dimensions. One of the themes of *Toxic Nourishment* is that there are people, perhaps all of us, perhaps not, who nourish themselves with toxic nourishment. They get what nourishment they can from emotional toxins. It's sort of like, perhaps I shouldn't say it, like flies living on fecal matter. One ekes out, one gets what nourishment one can from the awful environment one is in. And one's system gets used to getting nourishment that way. If a person somehow is in another context and you offer him something better, he can't use it. He can't use it because the equipment to use it hasn't developed. It's a problem in psychotherapy to offer something patients can't use. It actually shames the patient because you are taxing capacities that haven't arisen, that haven't developed. If a capacity to use good feelings from someone has not developed or developed well, therapy itself can be humiliating.

Therapy often faces the task of helping a person develop capacities that can use good feeling. This takes time, whether five years, ten years, twenty years. I have patients with me for forty years. Some of my first patients are with me. I think that would sound crazy to a normal person. What are they doing with you so long? What are you doing wrong? That is the wrong question to ask. There are some people who are so damaged and whose dependency needs are so damaged and so great, that it's like they need you to help them breathe. It's like you are the intensive care equipment. You help them breathe emotionally. You help them survive emotionally. One of Winnicott's great contributions to clinical work is that he didn't make patients feel guilty about dependency and rush them out. Let the dependency needs grow over time, flourish over time until they can actually use you. I think Winnicott contributes something culture needs, less shame over dependency.

I've long sensed a kind of moralism in Kleinian writings, a kind of shaming of patients. You're not good enough. You're paranoid-schizoid. You're not really good until you reach the depressive position. You're not grown up or fully human. You have to reach the depressive position. This seems to tax a capacity that needs support and time to develop and, even so, may not be the defining measure of a person.

In a Winnicottian approach, I feel more acceptance of an individual's lacks, more acceptance of the human being as he or she is, without shaming the person for what he isn't or can't be (assuming one knows or senses what he can be or should be). There's a danger in therapy of shaming the patient with his damaged psyche rather than support what is necessary to grow the capacity to go farther.

Maybe the patient will develop more of a false self to please the analyst, sort of like someone in jail who acts like they are not a thief anymore so they can get out of jail. I get a feeling that with a Winnicottian attitude there is a less judgmental sense of where the individual is, appreciation for the fully human struggle of this moment. You are not trying to rush them into something somewhere else. You support them from behind, so to speak, from below, atmospherically. Part of what comes through is an emotional presence, an emotional ambience that over time seeps in. You don't rub noses in deficiencies. You provide the atmosphere and gradually something happens. It's a different kind of supportive feeling, a kind of background support, rather than a persecuting feeling.

That's partly why Winnicott towards the end of his life said that interpretations aren't really that important. He feels that interpretations are more for the analyst than for the patient. And gradually it's almost as if he provides an invisible atmosphere that the patient lives in, a different kind of atmospheric possibility. But now we'll leave that behind and dip into Bion's world.

Bion in his own way has gone as deep or deeper than almost anyone exploring the psyche. There may be very few psychoanalysts that have reached the depths that Bion has. Donald Meltzer wrote that if you explore the psyche and try to go as far as you can, the chances are you will notice a little flag with the letter B already planted in the spot you are now coming upon. Chances are Bion has been there and moved on. He left a notation as if to say, "Ah! Here! Look at this. It is worth looking at." So much of Bion's work plants little flags in the psyche, little notations saying, "If you get here, stop a while. Take a look. It's worth taking in."

A writer like Bion, who seems to have barbed wire around him, isn't for everyone. But Winnicott isn't for everyone and Klein isn't for everyone. If they speak to you, you stay with it. If they don't speak to you, you find something that does speak to you. It's not worth wasting your time with something that doesn't speak to you. These writers speak to me. I only talk about writers I love, writers that have helped me, writers that have helped my search. I don't talk about writers that haven't helped me, that haven't gotten into me, that haven't lit me up and shown me who I am. I tell my students like I told the graduating class here yesterday, "Only read what is good for you. Only read what turns you on. Forget about the rest of the field. If something else comes your way, then it will come your way. But right now, read what you can read right now."

Onward to Bion. I'm going to focus on one little Bion clinical vignette. (Cogitations, 1992, p. 79; Eigen, 2004, pp. 62–67).

If you ever find a place in your being, a place in your psyche where barbed wire surrounds your soul and cuts into it, Bion may be waiting to help you. If you don't find that bloody place, you are lucky and you can go on safely without reading Bion.

Actually, I find Bion a deep kind of "fun", scary as he can be. One thing I enjoy is thinking about the vignettes he scatters through his work. I don't think he ever gives an extended case in his writings (unless you can call Bion himself an extended case in his autobiographies and in *Memoir of the Future*). Melanie Klein has. She wrote a narrative of her work with a child in psychoanalysis. A boy, Richard, during the Second World War, a detailed session-by-session book, well worth while (*Narrative of a Child Analysis*). Winnicott has sort of extended cases here and there, e.g., in *Playing and Reality* or *The Piggle*. There are chapters on this case or that case. But Bion doesn't. The most he has managed is little fragments, vignettes. It is not unusual for Bion to write in fragments, which add up, like a beam approaching a tumor at high intensity from different ways in.

The material I focus on this afternoon is from my Chapter "Half and Half" in *The Senstive Self*, which is about a Bion vignette drawn from his book, *Cogitations*. It involves a kind of British humour. There's a funny kind of humour in Bion, a black humour. It's invisible. It's almost as if he is making fun or mocking something. You don't know what he is mocking. Is he mocking himself? Is he mocking the patient? Is it ironical? It is very subtle. Is he mocking the psyche? Is he being ironical about the psyche? Is he being ironical about the human condition? What is he mocking? He is mocking our make up, what we are like. It is kind of a caricature, kind of like looking in the mirror, a funny mirror that is laughing at us. And it's our psyche that is laughing at us. And we look at it we say, "Is that who we are? I can't believe that is who we are."

He begins quoting a patient. A real patient? Something made up? Who knows? We never know how to evaluate these things, but what he portrays is part of psychic reality. In this vignette, he means to portray a certain sort of psychotic thinking. We are zeroing in on certain aspects of psychotic thinking. A lot goes on in psychosis, much of which we will not touch now. Bion here, as he often does, focuses on what I call "insectoid" aspects, something rigid, an external shell, crustacean. Something with very limited insides, so to speak.

Bion writes of a patient: "Well then, if you want to know," he said becoming confidential. "Last night I had a most enjoyable evening. People smoking, intelligent, friendly atmosphere. And then", becoming indignant in a noisy voice, "The waitress brought me only half a cup of coffee and that absolutely finished it." Dropping his voice, "I couldn't do a thing after that, not a thing," almost whispering, "That finished it." (*Cogitations*, p. 79).

This is a typical Bion fragment. What makes it up? A sudden change in experience from good to bad. Good dinner, things going nicely, having a most enjoyable evening. And then what happens? The waitress brings half a cup of coffee. That finished it. From good to bad, suddenly. The good can't be sustained, something spoils it, ruins it.

You see the therapist can't win. The therapist provides a half cup, something good enough in Winnicott's terms. Half a cup of coffee, it's OK. The therapist provides a decent enough idea or feeling. Not good enough for the individual here. Because it is not everything. The therapist didn't provide everything, and you know the truth is if the therapist by some horrible miracle were able to provide everything, that wouldn't be good enough either.

What I call 'the spontaneous recovery rhythm' is deficient, missing. We described a little earlier the baby going in and out of life in a natural kind of way. In the growth of Winnicott's clinical writings he understands the session to be like this. Something wrong happens, the therapist is seen to do something wrong. There is a breakdown. There is some kind of temporary breakdown. And if things keep on moving along ok there will be a spontaneous recovery in one form or another. So the sessions for Winnicott become breakdown, recovery, a breakdown, recovery rhythm, and here Bion is depicting this rhythm not working. There is just the breakdown and the capacity to recover from the breakdown is not there. The capacity to go in and out, back and forth, breakdown, become whole again. That capacity is damaged. It is not working.

Here the patient takes a hit. Something wrong happens. Something off happens and he goes under and recovery is not a possibility.

I had something like that in my life last night when I went home. My son and my wife went on a trip during the day, which is fine. And I went to the gym after the session yesterday, which is also very good. It felt good to move. Then I get a call from my wife and I believe she is at the train station and she tells me that they were going out for a bite to eat, which was fine. Then about an hour a two later they come back to the room and it turns out she called me from the hotel. And she and my son went out for dinner in the hotel after their day long trip and they didn't invite me. They didn't say, "Hey we're in the hotel. You want to join us?" My wife said in her mind she had somehow assumed that I had eaten already and that I didn't want to come. That was the picture in her mind. Whether negativity came from her or from me or both of us, I don't know. I was hurt like this man was hurt. I guess I thought they were calling from out of the hotel because they didn't say they were in the hotel. They didn't see me all day and now they go out to eat and they are in the hotel and they didn't even ask me if I want to join them.

I was feeling good up until that point. And then when they came in after dinner they looked good. They had a happy day, a great trip. Our son was very talkative. It was nice to hear him and listen to him and her. My wife was telling me about her experiences and inside me I was feeling hurt. I was feeling on the one hand, glad that they had a nice day and enjoying it and looking at what they were showing me. My pleasure was real. But there was this other sector, hurt that they didn't want to include me in their dinner plans. Internally, I was in great danger of ruining the evening.

One problem for me was how to express my hurt without damaging the evening or causing minimum damage. My wife saw me looking at her and knew exactly what was happening. I didn't have to say a word, she saw it and said, "You're hurt." And I said, "Yes, I'm hurt." And the hurt didn't go away so quickly. It took over and hour for it to go away. It couldn't go away until we had a chance to be together later and get to another level of feeling. So the recovery time, the recovery cycle wasn't immediate. I can't tell how much damage was done. Was there any damage or little damage or medium damage in this situation? But certainly the potential for damage was there. And although my recovery time took probably about an hour and a half, I think when I was younger it would have taken much longer.

Now my wife and I know that when she goes though her things and I go through my things, we know that recovery is possible. We've learned that over the decades we've been together. We've learned how to recover from ourselves. In the beginning it was more difficult. She kept breaking up with me and as time went on she decided to stay in the situation until I broke up with her, which never happened. So over time one of the things we learned, which we didn't have a capacity for in the beginning and which we had to develop the capacity for, was how to recover from ourselves, to recover from each other. And it took quite a long time learning. Children raise the stakes, intensify what's at stake. Always disruptions, always off balance. In contrast, Bion tells us about a man who cannot recover from himself. The capacity to recover from himself or from the other isn't there. He is stuck in a place where recovery is not a possibility. He says, "That finished it." The breakdown-recovery rhythm isn't working.

The patient dropping his voice makes me think of the kind of confidential "intimacy" a psychotic person can promote. When I first started working with psychosis I was in my twenties. I would be on a ward in a hospital and someone would come up to me saying, "You have a light? Do you have a cigarette?" And then he would start talking as if he were revealing the truth about something, something I needed to know. And then he would say, "You have to help me get out of here. I'm really sane. You have to help me get out of here." And he sounded very intimate. He would keep talking in an intimate way and in my young grandiosity I might feel, "Oh! Something is happening between us. An intimacy is happening between us. We are getting close." And then I realized he talked that way with everybody.

I felt something similar meeting homeless people when I was young. One of them came up to me in a very intimate way and said he needed money for a hamburger. I took him into the hamburger store a few steps away and ordered a hamburger and put the money on the counter. A few minutes later, I see him back out on the street asking for money for food again. I said, "I just bought you a hamburger. What happened?" He said, "I didn't have enough money for the tip, so I didn't get anything and left." He took the money on the counter and left.

Such experiences on the street and in the hospital taught me that a certain tone that sounds intimate is a signal that something funny may be happening. A signal saying, "You don't know what is happening. Better reserve judgment and wait and see."

In the Bion case we are looking at, life is being turned on and life is being turned off. Like a switch, on-off. The patient begins in an intimate, confidential way. 'Oh I was having a good time!' So in Kleinian terms we begin with a good breast. Something nourishing is happening. I was having a good evening. Life was nice. Everything was good. But in the psychotic mode this good feeling is usually followed by disaster. A disaster one can't recover from in any short time. It looks final. In psychosis disaster looks forever. I went down the tubes or I was in danger of going down the tubes yesterday. But I knew that it wasn't final. I've lived through enough to know that it is temporary. But in the psychotic mode it's now and it's forever. The experience is like it is for the baby. There is no time limit to it. It is forever. The hope is forever and the disaster is forever.

Nourishment is always wounded. A theme in Bion's work and Bion's clinical episodes is wounded nourishment (*Damaged Bonds*, Chapter Two, "Wounded Nourishment").

In a way, the picture, the clinical situation, is the opposite of what is normal for Winnicott. In Winnicott's clinical examples, life gets turned off and then back on. In this psychotic mode that Bion is trying to point us to, life is turned on and then it is turned off.

The turn-off hinges on an abrupt unexpected happening. A miscommunication often is involved, like with me last night. I had no idea that my wife and son were at the hotel. And from my wife's perspective she had no idea that I didn't know that for some reason. She didn't expect what I was experiencing and I didn't expect her reality. What happened was abrupt and unexpected. In all of Bion's cases this is the case. Something nice goes on and then an abrupt and unexpected happening, a spin into the negative. A bit like a Punch and Judy show. 'Hey, hey' in the beginning and then 'pow', everything changes quickly.

The waitress brings half a cup of coffee. How could she! How dare she! Does the patient think that she possesses diabolic intent? Is she merely careless, indifferent, inconsiderate, insensitive? Whether mean or distracted it is clear that she does not care enough. Her act is taken to reflect an uncaring, indifferent or wounding intention. Our psychoanalytic ear hears echoes of a wounding nourisher. We hear in the waitress a wounding nourisher even if it is a fantasy on the patient's part. We hear a wounded-wounding nourisher feeding the formation of personality. The personality as it is forming is being fed wounded nourishment. The personality forms feeding on wounds.

It's a slightly different nuance from Klein and Winnicott. It doesn't exclude Klein and Winnicott but is slightly different. The patient as a baby was fed wounds. The patient as a baby ate its own or another's wounds to nourish his psychophysical being.

Of course the wounding nourisher is the therapist, the analyst. The therapist is inevitably the wounding nourisher. This vignette is also about the therapist ruining things. The therapist's personality is always ruining things, unable to sustain a truly good situation.

A fusion of wound and nourishment runs through many of Bion's clinical portrayals. Here are a few examples to give you the flavour of this structure. In one, the patient reports having a good lunch. Again a good breast, a good feed, good nourishment, when unexpectedly, inexplicably a mug of beer is thrown in his face. In another example, Bion talks about the patient wanting ice cream only to reveal that what is happening in the patient is that whatever sweetness comes his way becomes part of an everlasting scream. The delight of ice cream becomes the scream of deprivation, fading into no scream at all as the patient dies into cold silence. Again, in another example, a patient's mother cuts off supplies. She doesn't want to pay for therapy anymore. Then the patient declares he doesn't have enough money to buy food, let alone the mental emotional food of analysis. All these examples cluster around potential nourishment or something sweet or maternal, and then something wrong happens, cuts off supplies, cuts off life, turns life off. In the example we are focusing on, the cup is half empty rather than half full. In psychic logic in the psychotic mode, half empty means more than totally empty.

Not totally full equals completely empty, nothing at all, less than nothing. For it is not simply nothing—nothing is OK, nothing is easy. But a hostile, furious, even malevolent nothing, a devastatingly insulting nothing. The patient feels insulted. And insult instantaneously spirals into devastation. Instead of just being insulted he is devastated. There are examples a little like this in Freud's dream book where people get blows to their ego, suffer blows to their ambition, insults to their self, and Freud describes their hurt, angry reactions. In the psychotic register, such blows and insults, real or imaginary, precipitate total devastation, black winter for endless time. Perceived insult equals assault equals devastation. Experience gets negatively infinitized. Less than everything equals less than nothing. And less than nothing is infinitely worse than nothing.

The half empty cup example conveys a sense of finality, absolute finality. In certain forms of schizophrenic and depressive experience absolute becomes a sense of doom. Often in psychosis an individual feels that he has made a fatal mistake or failed to act bravely enough in following the true path, that he has sealed a bargain with the devil and is doomed forever. Change is not possible although a longing for salvific change never quite goes away. The sense of doom and salvific longing are strange attractors and go together.

At the doom level of experience, the psychotic tone is tinged with hysteria, panic, is deadly serious yet also mocking. This is buried in Bion's example, in which the tone is lighter in a blackish sort of way. I think I hear the mocking, the contempt, the reference to repetitious damnation. The passage has a funniness too. Is it Bion's tone? The patient's supercilious attitude? What is he purveying as disaster? Bion's examples always refer to catastrophic shock. Disaster at the beginnings of personality formation. Here he has a kinship with Winnicott. He touches some kind of deformation as personality begins to form. A catastrophic shock, big bang, a smash, an explosion at the beginning of personality. A half empty cup or breast, a feed that went wrong, hints at much more than a bad or unsuccessful nursing situation. In part, it hints at something missing. Something missing in life, something not there in life itself and in the capacity for life even as it nourishes and wounds. This is so in the best of situations and much more so in the worst. Fusions of lack and damage.

The patient is reporting the ongoing disaster of his being, the ongoing disaster of his life. A sense of disaster that has hardened around him, molded him, encased him. This patient we are speaking of can't live outside this deforming disaster.

We left off with the patient reporting, depicting, expressing, trying to show, but not necessarily communicating. He does what he does over and over and over again. He perseverates. His thinking is obsessive. Psychotic thinking often has hysterical emotions and obsessive thoughts as well as a schizoid dimension. It mimics communication but the latter is often stillborn, inundated by obsessive repetition.

It is tempting to give meaning to psychotic imagery. It may seem packed with meaning and in fact may be so. Yet Bion makes us aware of another dimension, an underlying problem. Whatever psychotic imagery can mean (mythic, cosmic, personal or transpersonal), is overshadowed by the fact that a catastrophe is signaled. That is, what is produced is less a symbol than a signal, a showing. The individual is showing, signaling a state of disaster. A therapist might want to analyze archetypal imagery and trace self progression. But Bion says what may be happening is that the psychotic is saying over and over and over again, "Catastrophe in progress. Catastrophe in progress. I'm a catastrophe. Life is a catastrophe." "Help me! Help me!" going on and on, repeatedly flashing a catastrophic message without making contact. The psychotic subject is stuck in a relentless mold, as if saying over and over, "My insides are a disaster but I don't have insides to process it. My insides are catastrophic but I don't have insides to work with the catastrophe."

As if the psyche is evacuating itself in the psychosis. All this imagery, all these fireworks going off may be the psyche trying to get rid of itself. Maximum-minimum emotion oscillating with flashes of deadness. As if the psyche is too much for itself. It's too painful to have a psyche. It's too painful to be a psychic being. It's too catastrophic and I have nothing, nothing, nothing in me to work with it.

Bion's patients, in general, were eternally getting half a cup of coffee and feeling hopeless about it. In one or another form, they keep getting a half cup and keep experiencing worse than nothing.

I personally, don't see any difference between internal disaster and external disaster. Between what happens in Iraq, what happens in Palestine, what happens inside us. It's all part of the great human disaster, what we do to ourselves, what happens to us, and our inability to process what we go through.

Sometimes Bion feels that we have to make something very, very bad happen outside, something horrible happen outside so we can begin to feel the impact that our insides are having on us. Nevertheless a real disaster is being conveyed. A disaster as great as soul or self or world destruction. An apocalypse now, ongoing. A forever apocalypse. It's a basic psychotic state. It is as if the personality dies and comes back mummified or encrusted, encrusted with this catastrophic dread. Semi-undead enough to keep on reporting, but not really able to do much about it.

Psychotic language is like an SOS in progress. It's like an SOS, disaster in progress. I have become a crustacean or insect or exoskeleton in order to live with the disaster in progress. The fact that I have become that is part of the disaster also. But somehow there is still a sensitivity. The black box in the crash still sends signals—the half empty cup tale, the story of sensitivity wounded, the inability to respond. The patient reports sensitivity dramas without the ability to go through them. It's the sensitivity that keeps on getting scraped but is unable to go through the experience. He points a finger at the wound and the wounder and says, "Look what you've done! Look what you've done to me!" and he stops there. When he says, "That finished it!" He refers not only to an underlying sense of finality, not only the closing off of recovery, but also the closing off of the possibility of recovering from life. Life always is going to remain too much of a disaster that can't be recovered from.

He repeats over and over the moment of closing down going on forever, incessant absolute finality. Cure partly involves moving from reporting to bearing witness. The psychotic reports his news. Disaster in progress, analysis as disaster. All his cells and pores and being report it. Yet he does not bear witness. He can not work with it. He is not fully touched by himself. It is as if he flashes his disastrous state on a screen but can not take it in and be moved. The therapist must grow to bear witness to it, give it a place, supply a context, supply big Buddha ears feel it, provide a place in the world for it.

The psychotic with the half filled cup shows how important feelings are by what does not happen to them. They are not taken in, they are not suffered, not processed, not digested; rather, they are spewed out over and over. The therapist doesn't do the reporting. The therapist is the one who feels the impact, who takes in the impact, in doses as much as one can stand. You fall asleep in session. You turn off in session. You do what you need to do to survive in the session. But along with that, little by little over time you begin to feel the impact of who this person is, what the truth of the person is. You begin to feel it and bear witness to it in a way the person himself can't. You become an auxiliary catastrophe processor because the person can't process it himself. Do our feelings count? I think Bion's half cup episode shows they do quite a lot, even if access to them is severely limited.

Dialogue with audience

Question 1

This is a comment. Yesterday I felt a cry within myself. What was it? Was it the baby's scream towards the mother? While I was having this thought you were saying, "Scream, scream" and although I could not understand you well I felt that you were responding to my desperate inner scream. I would like to thank you for opening my ears to the disappearing scream of the baby and for holding that baby before I could. Thank you to whoever that was. That is exactly what makes this worthwhile for me that I am here to serve that infant and feel blessed that I had a chance to do that even a little bit with one person.

Response 1

Thank you.

Question 2

I wanted to scream but I could not and I often had night terrors. Fortunately, through analysis the night terrors have stopped. But does the wounded infant who wants to scream remain in one's heart?

Response 2

Yes, the scream remains. The wounded infant with the scream in its heart is with us till the end of days. But when our world gets larger the scream occupies less space. Traumas never go away but they take up less room. Other things become more interesting. A little like Winnicott's description of a transitional object. It remains in the unconscious but loses meaning. Other things become more meaningful as one grows. Similarly, the wounded self has influence. It doesn't go away. There are going to be many more wounds ahead. Sometimes I think the wounds in adulthood are worse than the wounds in infancy. Although the wounds in infancy form the infant, there is much more resiliency, more elasticity than later in life. Something bad can happen to a grown-up and have such impact that the person has a heart attack and dies. This is less likely to happen in infancy, although chronic toxic or emotionally under-nourishing conditions can be disastrous too.

At some point in my thirties or forties, I got tired of talking about my problems. I started getting bored by them. That didn't mean that they went away or that they didn't have a lasting effect on my personality organization, the kind of person I am. They continued but they bored me and other things were more interesting. For me now, without much time to live, what is more interesting for me is saying goodbye to myself. It has opened up new fields of experience. I am going to say goodbye me. And it's made life very different. Whole new worlds are opening up for me. It's astonishing, all the fields of experience that open up in life. I remember once I discovered a little doll I used to play with when I was a child. I think I made it when I was in kindergarten. I think I sewed it and stuffed it with cotton and I loved it. It was so meaningful to me. When I saw it as a teenager it was empty. It had no emotional coloration. I felt, "Oh my god! Is that what I loved so much?" It's the same with our problems and the way in which we are invested in them. The personality is glued to them, fixed to them. On the one hand the problems have molded us and have had a real effect. On the other hand they have attracted our attention and we are fixed on them. We have given them energy. We have given them coloration. They don't have to last forever, not so compellingly. One keeps growing and one can outgrow something of their hold.

Question 3

If the paranoid-schizoid position and the depressive position are defenses, can phantasy also be a defense against pain?

Response 3

The short answer to the question is anything can be used to defend against anything else. That is part of our plasticity and part of our rigidity. It is what enables us to survive in any condition, even to survive in hell. We can survive almost anything psychically and physically. What we also have is rigidity. A capacity that enables us to survive in one situation sinks us in another. An example that Bion gives in *Memoir of the Future,* one of his last books, a kind of play, a drama, a reverie. He wrote it in California, which maybe freed him to do it, a new or another way of writing psychoanalysis. He gave expression to different parts of the psyche and society, different tendencies. A three part work. In one section he writes of the tyrannosaurus and stegosaurus. The stegosaurus developed impressive armour that enabled it to survive in its environment but worked against its survival when the environment changed. Same thing with tyrannosaurus. The tyrannosaurus developed properties that enabled it to survive in one condition and when conditions changed it failed to survive. Life changes and what works in a set of circumstances can boomerang in another.

So far our plasticity, or interaction of plasticity and rigidity, enabled us to survive in a wide variety of conditions. Part of our ability to survive involved ability to defend ourselves mentally as well as physically. A fear now has to do with the momentum technology has in our age, which enabled us to evolve new versions of tyrannosaurus-stegosaurus properties, technologies which are extensions of our brain-mind. Not only are the physical conditions of life changing, the mental conditions of our life are changing too. The way we use technology and our brain-mind can destroy us or bring us to new places. In the Bible, God keeps asking, Where are you? I'm not sure anyone's come up with a good answer as yet.

Question 4

How did you and your wife learn to recover from each other in marriage?

Response 4

Just lucky. I married late in life, forty five. My wife and I had been on and off for quite a while before we stayed together. I don't know who broke up with who most. Maybe I had enough of the single life. I wrote about some of my experiences in *Lust,* as well as lust's work in human culture. Maybe I just got old enough to see that time is real. A big factor was my wife stopped breaking up with me. She got the idea that I was provoking her to break up, so she determined to outwait me, telling herself, "He'll have to be the one to break up. I'm not going to do it for him." Some kind of wall gave way and we found ourselves on the other side of it. Now the true challenges began. If we were going to stay together we had to learn how to modulate at least some of the ways we caused each other and ourselves pain. If we were going to stay together, we would have to do something about our need to inflict pain. Something had to be done or it would be a disaster.

If you're single and seeing this person or that, you don't have to do that much to change yourself. You don't have to seriously struggle with yourself beyond a certain point. You break up, it's over, someone else appears sooner or later. But if you are living together and want to make a go of it, you realize you have a lot of work to do in order to share the same space. You are called to account. You can't get away with coasting. I think it took me awhile to catch on. I was unprepared for how alone I felt in my marriage at certain points. More alone than ever. How could this be? I thought marriage solved aloneness. When one marries one expects not to be alone. "It's done. We're together, sharing the same space. That's it. Now I will never feel alone again." All of a sudden you realize, "My god! There's another person here!" The other person has a will, a mind, a life of her own. One that is capable of frustrating expectations and making you feel alone. I thought about that a lot and at some point realized my expectations about living with someone else were crazy. My expectations, my semi-conscious picture of what a relationship *should* be like, put too great a burden on the actual relationship. I had to do something about modulating the kind of stranglehold my mind had on me and me on it, as to who I thought my wife should be, what kind of person she was—the stranglehold my mind had on the person I pictured inside it. The stranglehold was more imaginary than real but it had real effects. In reality, my wife went her own way and did her own thing, and her living her own life feeling helped me immensely. It forced me to learn to make room for another, for a fuller me. Perhaps the single most important thing that helped was the love I felt for our children. I never felt that much love before and love changed me little by little. I started seeing my patients differently. I started seeing them as my children. And I started feeling the preciousness of every human being. Little by little, I was transformed by love. I'm far from perfect—I think you've seen that. I've shared myself with you. I'm still a mess. I'm a little less dangerous. It's not simply learning how to modulate your hurtful aspects, although that's part of it. It's being transformed inside by a feeling you didn't expect to have.

Question 5

You mentioned that there were several types, nuances of screaming. Is acting out also one of them and if so, how is it different?

Response 5

Always, it is. Acting out can have many ingredients including some kind of screaming. What kind? You have to use your intuition. You can do exercises keep a notebook. Meditate on acting out and what it makes you feel, either you are acting out or someone else is acting out. Write it all down. See what comes to you and use your imagination and reverie. Whatever acting out you are thinking of, try to listen to it. Sit with it, be quiet and give it time to reverberate in you and take notes. It's like going on a psychedelic trip. You sit with an experience you sit with an action. Stay two weeks sitting with your question, feeling the acting out and taking notes on it. Whatever comes to you, stay with it. See what you come up with and you will get something interesting, I assure you.

Question 6

Thank you for your explanation about how the scream precedes splitting. Although screaming is not a rigid dichotomy like splitting, I had the thought that it might be a more flexible dichotomy because one requires an object to listen to the scream. Can we differentiate between splitting and screaming according to the dichotomy?

Response 6

Winnicott talks about this in his book, *Human Nature* (1990). But I will try to say something about it. For different, overlapping reasons, Winnicott and Bion are discontent with Klein's theory of the paranoid-schizoid and depressive positions. Bion feels there are more formless states before splitting. Winnicott talks about what he calls primary aloneness, an aloneness supported by an unknown infinite other (the first two chapters of *Flames from the Unconscious: Trauma, Madness and Faith* (2009) focus on Winncott's primary aloneness). The alone one needs support for aloneness without knowing it. The infant receives support it does not know it's getting. The quality of unknown background support varies, and how it varies affects how we feel. Like barometric pressure. If you look at a barometer, it's always oscillating back and forth. It's not steady. It vibrates. And in the same way, emotional life is not steady, not static. It is always vibrating like weather.

As the unknown support varies, the way the infant feels varies. The psychic atmosphere of the moment changes the emotional world of the infant without the latter being aware of how this is happening. There is no idea of splitting or not splitting here. It is more amorphous, nebulous, interweaving. It involves permeability. We are permeable. Emotional osmosis works between us. We transmit from mind to mind, feeling to feeling directly, instantaneously. No barrier. As time goes on, we erect barriers. Barriers grow. We have to erect barriers to stand up in the world, so to speak. Winnicott depicts a time or psychic thread before inner or outer space is developed in such a way that splitting can be relevant.

In Melanie Klein's formulation, splitting too is interactive or enters interactive fields through projection-introjection. I project myself into the other and introject the other into myself, an ongoing, back and forth process. But what Winnicott is saying is there are domains of being before splitting. For now, let's say there is a permeability in the way we support or fail to support each other. Feelings are transmitted back and forth, feeding our psyche, a feeling atmosphere, psychic air we breathe, our psychic oxygen.

One more thing. It's about Winnicott's patient who we talked about in the morning session, the woman who had to dream her scream, who felt the realness of her dream scream, and so felt real too. Winnicott writes that she began to sing in analysis after she encountered her dream scream. She had not been able to sing before and now became a singer. It is wondrous to experience transformations that go on if we don't get in the way too much.

CHAPTER THREE

Day 3

Morning session: Murder and coming through

Thank you for coming back today. It's hard to believe it's already the last day. Although we don't understand each other's language, I feel a deep bond with the people I've met in Korea, a soul bond. It seems like there are less and less people everyday, but those who came today are here to get more. A couple of people said how hard Bion is for them, and that maybe someday they will be able to get into it. My recommendation, if you are interested in trying, is to start with his seminars. He has the Tavistock seminars (2005), the Italian seminars [2005], the Paris seminar [2000], and another seminar, the one I attended, is called Bion in New York and Sao Paolo [1980]. My favourite of his seminars, perhaps for the essays that the book includes afterwards, is the Clinical Seminars and Other Works [1994]. A sentence I like a lot in the beginning of the paper, "Making the Best of a Bad Job," is "When two people meet, an emotional storm is created." (p. 1994, p. 321; Eigen 2005, p. 17). This sentence became the basis of my book, *Emotional Storm*, in which, among other things, I link aspects of Bion with Buber, Levinas and Wittgenstein.

Many years ago the poet Robert Frost was asked about speed-reading, which became a craze in the United States for a while. Speed-reading helped businessmen go through vast amounts of material in a short time. Instead of courses on speed-reading, which universities were beginning to teach as the burden on students increased, Robert Frost said that he wanted to give a course on how to read more slowly. Speed and quantity ruined education. My feeling is if you can get one sentence out of a book that changes your life or stays with you or influences you or makes you think or makes you feel that book was worthwhile, just savour that sentence. When I was in my twenties, I chanced upon a sentence in a book by Thomas Merton, a simple sentence that changed my life. The sentence is, "The secret of our identity is in the divine mercy of God." These words changed me. Something touched me and everything changed.

One thing that baffles me since I've been here. Before I came here I kept looking for a book a Korean analyst once gave me, which I read a long time ago. I know I have the book. I am almost certain that I gave it to one of my sons, but so much gets lost in the vast and changing sea of books that accumulate. What most impressed me in this book, and it may be that I misread it, was that the author talked about a word. I don't remember the word. It's a Korean word for a certain kind of soul malady. It was a beautiful book about a certain kind of soul sickness. When I was invited to give these talks I searched for that book and I kept wondering if the person who gave me that book fifteen years ago or so, after a talk I gave in New York City, would be here. I thought about this beautiful book on and off through the years. The man is sitting here now and he happens to have founded this institute, Jae hoon Lee. I looked for him on the Internet. I wrote him a note about it. He didn't respond. He didn't say, "Yes, I'm the one who wrote that book." Then I came here and we started talking. It turns out that yes, he is the man who wrote the book and gave it to me fifteen years ago when we were both fifteen years younger. Why it's not in Korean, I don't know. Maybe you can find out because I tried to find out and failed. You would think it would be a primary text for the institute he founded and I hope to catalyze that. Maybe I'm embarrassing him and he has reasons of his own for not having translated it into Korean, but maybe you can help solve this mystery.

I don't want to embarrass Jae hoon too much. I think he has done a beautiful thing in founding this institute. I find the people here very, very good seekers of what we are all looking for. Every institute has its problems, of course. But the commitment here I feel is very real and very heartening.

Now I promised to talk about murder today and that's what I am going to do. But there are a lot of things left over. A few questions kept coming up about Winnicott's scheme and how splitting fits in. I stopped teaching that many years ago but I'll try to become a teacher again, at least a little bit, and try to go over something like a chronology for Winnicott even though it is against the grain of Winnicott and certainly against my grain. I think it will be worthwhile to get some kind of skeleton on some of Winnicott's early ideas.

I've written about murder all through my work. And for Winnicott and Bion murder is an extremely important topic. For Melanie Klein of course. I have an essay on suicide in *Toxic Nourishment* that mainly focuses on young people in their teens and twenties. There is a chapter also on the pressure that children feel from busy parents. Busy parents, busy children. So I write about familial and social pressures relating to suicide in *Toxic Nourishment*.

In *Emotional Storm,* I write an autobiographical essay about killers and dreams. You get killers in dreams a lot. You get break-ins and you have murderers you are afraid of in your dreams. You're going to get killed, you're going to get broken into. It's a basic dread. In *Emotional Storm* I also have a chapter called 'The urge to kill oneself.' So I write about killers, the urge to kill and the urge to kill oneself.

In the *Sensitive Self* I have a chapter called 'A Basic Rhythm.' (pp. 18–35) A basic rhythm is something I talked about yesterday. 'A' basic rhythm, not 'the' basic rhythm. I once gave a talk years ago for Jungians in the Wild West in a beautiful setting in the United States. I was talking about what Bion calls the force that goes on working after it destroys existence, time, space and personality. A British Jungian, Fred Plaut said, "Not 'the', 'a'. It's not "the" force that goes on working after it destroys time, space, personality and existence, its "a" force that goes on working." So I went back and read Bion and yes, there it was. It says 'a' force, not 'the' force. It sounds like a little thing. But try saying 'a' instead of 'the.' We have a tendency to make grand statements. This is 'the' instead of this is 'a.' This is 'a' factor among other factors. This is 'a' factor among many qualifying factors. So there is no 'the.' There are lots of 'a's. Language skews our thinking, molds our thinking into making these grand absolute pronouncements when we are really just talking about a little but important factor in a mass of important factors. A force that goes on working after it destroys life, personality, space, time, existence.

In Chinese there is its complement, Kwan Yin, a compassionate force. I don't know the Korean name for her, I'm going to need help. In Japan it was Kannon. I saw on the streets and in the museum here the same figure, but I don't know the name of this Buddhist helper in Korean. Kwan Yin can't do anything except be compassionate. It's her nature. What gift does she ask in return for responding to your heart's desires? Can anyone guess what she wants in return? All she wants is for you to say thank you. She gives what's in her to give. It's a principle in the soul, heart, mind, and being. Her essence is to be giving. The Kwan Yin in us can't do anything but give. What Bion talks about is a parallel force, Kwan Yin's alternate, opposite, complement: a force that can't do anything but destroy. A force that goes on destroying after it destroys everything that can be destroyed. It feeds off destruction. It feeds off nothing. It feeds off whatever is or isn't.

There's a general point I want to make this morning so I might as well make it quickly. Then I will be free to do whatever I feel like. It's a simple point. In Winnicott an emphasis is on the other. He calls it the object in old philosophical language. In one of his breakthrough accounts, the use of object account, his emphasis is on the other surviving me. The other surviving my destructiveness. And he means the other survives my destructiveness in an intact way. It's not easy to do because you get scared, you draw back, you regroup. In reality, I might tell a patient, "I guess I didn't survive you very well this session. But I'll be back again tomorrow or next week. Give me a little time and I'll reappear." Winnicott has a picture of the object surviving one's destruction in a spontaneous way. One retains one's spontaneous being and responds in a non-retaliatory fashion. Usually aggression is met with aggression. You retaliate. If it goes on a long time you want revenge over a longer period of time. I remember a state I would get into when I was little child with my father: "You wait until I get older. I'll get my revenge. I'll get back at you." And it smolders. Normally we meet aggression with aggression. And if we're helpless in the situation we think of the future. "Alright. You'll get yours in the time to come. Even if it's in hell after life."

I think of the biblical suggestion to turn the other cheek. Winnicott's idea is a little better formulated. It fills in some of the details. Winnicott was brought up in a Wesleyan family and imbibed Wesleyan principles and emotional states. They find their way into his concepts, e.g., the holiness of the vital spark. Winnicott tries to trace a vital spark as a thread through development. He has a Wesleyan notion of how to respond to another human being no matter what the other human being is doing. This kind of religious or spiritual background plays a role in Winnicott's thinking, perhaps more than one might realize. Another example, one of his great formulations is the idea of an incommunicado core. A core that is supported by an unknown, boundless, infinite other, a background sense of boundless infinite support. An unknown core of our being. It comes from his quietist upbringing, but he does a lot more filling in of the psychological details. It may be that religions often formulate where to go, but don't always fill in how to get there fully enough. Buddhism probably gives it the best shot as a psychology that is detailed in covering just about everything. But it seems to miss some points of emphasis when it comes to where real people are at. It works for some. It doesn't work for others, like everything else. It works in some ways; it doesn't work in other ways. What I want to focus on now are some of the psychological ins and outs of Winnicott's basically spiritual formulation. (I write about Winnicott's primary aloneness and unknown, boundless support in the first two chapters of Flames *from the Unconscious: Trauma, Madness and Faith*).

For Winnicott so much in development hinges on how the other responds to our destructiveness. He might say that this destructiveness is more than just aggression against an object. It's more than just I'm angry at you. It's not that. That's too little, too defined. I'm mad at you. It's not like that. I think that in part, when Winnicott talks about this destructiveness that we are called upon to survive in a responsive way, without losing our natural spontaneity, that destructiveness is what Bion is talking about by a force that destroys everything and goes on destroying everything even after it has destroyed everything, that feeds on its own destruction. You can get glimpses of this in babies when they can't stop screaming. When no matter what you do, they go on screaming. You don't know why they are screaming. Is it just physical distress? Are they seeing a devil? It's like whatever it is that is going on feeds on itself. It has its own momentum. It can't stop. You get it in little ways, say with a colicky baby when it feeds upon its own irritation. It can't stop because the irritation feeds on itself. You can get glimpses of what Bion is talking about here. And I feel that this kind of massive destructive force is the complement of Kwan Yin, a complement that goes on and on. How we respond to it determines the quality of lived experience. Much hinges on the quality of response. It's a profoundly religious understanding of how to respond to aggression in human life. It certainly isn't practical. It certainly isn't political. It certainly isn't normal. But Winnicott says everything depends on it.

After saying that our ideal is that the other survives our destructiveness in an integral spontaneous way, I must also quickly say that it is very real. There are gradations in the way we respond to each other's negativity or respond to each other's destructiveness. You can see that some people do it spontaneously better than others. You can see that some people aren't that threatened by their baby's all out energy, all out rage. A mother will protect herself so she won't get hurt by him, she is not going to get willingly hurt. She will say "ouch". But there is a difference in the way one does that depending on one's spontaneous nature, one's spontaneous attitude. Winnicott talks about a thought experiment. He talks about the possibility of being born into two different worlds.

In one world the infant kicks the mother. The mother doesn't like being kicked or hurt and will stop the infant from hurting her and will do what she needs to do to protect herself from pain. But you can do that in different ways. One mother will protect herself but feel a certain pleasure. Glad the baby is alive and kicking. Likes to see her baby thrive. Just needs not to get hurt by it. There is no moralistic attitude about its kicking nature. It's the baby's spontaneity and she feels pleasure that her baby is alive and well and kicking. That is one situation. In the other situation, the other world, the infant kicks the mother, say he tries to kick the mother's breast. This mother not only draws back, but conveys a moralistic attitude to the baby. 'Kicking is wrong. Kicking is bad.' And it may not be anything that is said, but it's something that is felt or seen, and is transmitted as an emotional atmosphere. This response goes right into the baby and the baby feels bad about being an alive kicking being. In one instance, the mother protects herself but affirms the baby's life feeling and in another instance the mother protects herself and makes the baby feel bad about being alive.

In the first example, the mother liked the baby's aliveness but doesn't want to get hurt by it, she is doing what Winnicott describes as surviving the baby's destructiveness while maintaining herself as a whole person, as a whole spontaneous alive human being. In this case aliveness speaks to aliveness. There isn't a break in being, so to speak. In the second instance, the mother can't respond, doesn't respond to the baby's destructive attacks. And what are the destructive attacks? We get some insight from this example that tells us how very often the destructive attacks are part of the life feeling, part of our feeling alive. When a two-year old starts throwing things around the house and breaking things, it can be part of his life feeling. Destruction can be part of aliveness for Winnicott. How does one respond to it? By saying, "Oh that's terrible! That's bad!" Or somehow, "Don't do that but I appreciate your being alive." It's a difference in qualities of being that he is addressing. And it is very real and we realize it in different ways. (See *Psychic Deadness* and *The Sensitive Self* for more on this paradigm).

Now I'll take it a step further. The first mother in all likelihood is not going to be perfect. But my hunch is that the way Winnicott is depicting her she'll be the kind of mother that the baby can forgive. The devoted good mother doing her best—protecting herself, protecting the baby, protecting her aliveness, protecting the baby's aliveness. She is doing her best whatever her limits are. She is not a know-it-all. She is responsive, caring, has her flaws, tries to work within her limits. In basketball you hear announcers talking on the TV describing a certain basketball player as working within his limits, playing within his limits. It's a good thing. He is not playing outside himself or playing beyond himself. He is not going to trip himself up by doing what he can't do. He is doing what he can do. And this first mother does what she can do and does her best. There is a certain humility. There is a certain self-care and a certain protection of the infant's vitality. She is the sort of person that the infant can forgive for her inevitable failings. The possibility of forgiving (it happens non-verbally) is not a cognitive thing, it's a soul thing. It's a soul feeling. It's the way life feels. These are different ways that life feels. What this therapy is about and what this developmental view is about is how life feels to the baby, how life feels to the mother. It is very important for the universe because if life feels really bad to people, the universe is going to be a bad universe. If life feels OK to people, it is going to be a much better universe.

I began as a therapist working with children. Then in clinic work I had both children and adult patients. I started off with disturbed children. First with schizophrenic and autistic children and children with behaviour disorders. Maybe that's part of what got me into schizophrenia and psychosis. When I started clinic work later in my twenties, I worked with adults too. When I worked with kids in a clinic setting I began to wonder why I kept getting hurt and injured, physically injured? I don't advise you to do the things I did. I was too crazy and loose. If a kid wanted to climb on the garage at the clinic, we'd go out climb a tree, get on the garage, dance around, and make believe we were Tarzan or something. We did all kinds of crazy things. And I got injured. I would be going beyond my limits. Eventually, after getting hurt for a few years, I began to realize I was over-extended. I would over-extend myself in the session. I would get drawn in by the appeal of the other, the demand of the other, the injury of the other. The child appealed for healing and made demands out of that appeal and I tried to fulfill them. Then I would get hurt. So I had to learn little by little to draw back and work within my limits. I began to develop a signal system. I could feel a signal inside. 'Uh oh. This is going to be trouble. You are going beyond what you can do. You are going to be beyond what you are comfortable with. You are going to get hurt.' So the raw fact of physical injury led me to develop a signal system inside to know when I was going too far and when I needed to protect myself.

I wondered what do people do who don't climb on roofs with their child patients? Not every child therapist climbs on roofs. My wife doesn't climb on roofs with her patients. I am thinking about a particular kid at the moment. Two or three different kids are coming back to mind now. I liked their energy. I did nutty things with some kids on an energy level. I remember a school for disturbed kids. I worked with a little withdrawn boy there who didn't speak and saw that he was attracted to the big boys playing basketball. So I decided he should be free to be on the court while the big boys are playing basketball. All the teachers were saying, "That's crazy. Big boys are going to kill him.

He is going to get injured." And in this particular case he went on the court with the big boys and they took care of him. They somehow responded to him. They took care of him spontaneously. They saw he was small and maybe saw something else, something about him, and they worked with him, worked around him, humoured him. Often they just ignored him and played their game. And within a year he began to talk. So you never know whether you should follow your urge or you should not follow your urge. The acceptance of the energy level somehow did enliven him. The communication was that energy is good and that *his* energy was good. His energy is as good as the big boys. It was a different kind of communication.

Now with the boy that I kept getting hurt with, or with some of the boys I kept getting hurt with, I had to learn how to say, "No, we can't do that but we can to this. We can't do X but we can do Y." Gradually as I began inside to protect myself I began to integrate a positive feeling towards substitutions. It's OK to substitute. Especially if it grows from an internal feeling like Winnicott's patient's singing grows out of her scream. She is not going to have access to this primitive level in a full, all-out way. It is being channeled, spontaneously finding a stream of life. It's Winnicott's interest to protect this stream, this thread of life through our development, to help nourish this thread, enable it to survive, to survive our own selves and survive the selves of others. So how one says "No" is very important. A self-protective function is very important. Saying "no" does not go against responding well to the other's aggression, or to the other's destructive tendency, or simply to the other's life energy. I used to feel that when I was dating lots of girls a good 'No' is better than a bad 'Yes.' There were ways that girls could say "No" that would make me feel good and ways that their acquiescence or "yes" was really not very enlivening. So it depends on the spirit.

I once was in therapy with Dorothy Bloch. Since I was alone in a room with a woman, I felt it incumbent upon me to try to seduce her. She should come on the couch with me. So there was a period when I gave it a try, trying to get Dorothy to lie down with me on the therapy couch. And I marvel at how she got out of it without hurting my feelings. It was something I thought about years afterwards. How did she do that? She would always somehow get out of it and make me feel good. That was an art, part of what Winnicott was talking about by the other's response to one's energy. It would have been destructive if we had slept together. When one's libido isn't innocent, libido causes a lot of difficulty. I still don't know how she did it. It was beautiful. It was beautiful to see how graceful and invisible psychoanalysis can be.

Doing therapy gives us a chance, gives us a privilege, to refine something in our selves. I don't know if it is our energy. I don't know if we refine our energy. I wouldn't exactly say that. But we develop our sensitivity, slight nuances of feeling. A certain refinement of psychic taste buds, a sense of how life feels. We become what Rilke calls bees of the invisible: *'We are bees of the invisible. We madly gather the honey of the visible to store it in the great golden hive of the invisible.'* (*Duino Elegies*), and sometimes it is seamless, you don't see the stitches. What Dorothy did with me in that instance, I didn't see the stitches. It was like a samurai's 'Swish' except it was gentle. It just happened from her nature and I don't know how she did it. But I learned from it the necessity of how to say 'No' in a way that affirms the other person.

It just occurred to me that this word 'No' that I am using is almost a crude masculine form of what I'm trying to express. Because Dorothy Bloch never used the word, 'No' with me. She somehow slipped out of the situation. She never used the word, 'No.'

Interpreter: Just a while ago, someone gave me a gift to give to Dr. Eigen. All of you in the audience may not be able to see it—it is an engraving of Kwan Yin. She had been carrying it in her wallet as a good luck charm for many years and wants you to have it. In Korean, Kwan Yin is Kwan Eum (bo sal).

Thank you. I hope it is OK for me to take this and I hope that it increases the luck and blessings for both of us, for all of us.

Winnicott's idea about surviving the destructive urges of the infant in an intact way may sound a bit abstract or idealized, but it has very real applications, very real consequences in everyday life. It emphasizes the quality with which we respond to the other's affect. Some of you have patients with very difficult affect and some of you may not. I tried to talk about the two worlds an infant can be born into in a more or less everyday way and make a parallel with that and patients in therapy. What I am trying to bring to attention is the importance of how we survive our patient's destructive urges.

Some of you have talked to me and said they don't have patients that destructive and some people said they do. Whether you do or don't, the quality of affect in our response matters. In the second situation, the moralistic mother, the one who feels that she is going to get killed by the baby's kick, by the baby's life force, that the baby's aliveness is going to kill her, responds condemningly. She makes the baby draw back, inhibited, afraid of his life force because the mother feels it's bad. This mother, I suspect, is a know-it-all. She knows everything. She seems to know what is good for the baby in a way that is bad for the baby. So this is a special kind of omniscience. She thinks she knows what is right for the baby. She thinks she knows what is right about life. And what she thinks is good for the baby turns out to be bad for the baby. But the baby doesn't necessarily know that.

Some time ago, when the cold war between the United States and Russia was the big thing in our world, or at least in my part of the world, my big fear was that someone would push the button to start atom bombing the other, thinking they knew something that they didn't. In *The Psychotic Core* I described such a situation as miscalculation from the viewpoint of omniscience. Thinking one knows it all, thinking one knows something one doesn't, one miscalculates about reality. Thinking one knows more than one knows about what the other is up to is horrendously dangerous in such a situation.

In *The Psychotic Core* I have chapters on omnipotence and omniscience. Psychoanalysts have written a lot about omnipotence, but not too much about omniscience. Bion has made important observations about omniscience and Donald Meltzer, who is a fan of Bion's, made some very good observations. Meltzer is one of the two or three most creative Kleinians. After you read the Kleinian basics and want to read the most creative Kleinians, try Donald Meltzer and Ignacio Matte-Blanco. Next to Bion, they are the most creative Kleinians I've read. In the United States, there is a thread of ferment of Klein-Bion work, pockets of creativity, e.g. James Grotstein, Harold Boris, Tom Ogden. Henry Elkin, also in the United States, wrote important passages on omniscience.

I am postulating that the second mother, the moralistic mother, thinks she knows more about the infant than she really does, and is acting against the infant's best interest on the basis of this imaginary knowledge. This is the mother that the infant can't forgive. The first mother I talked about is forgivable. She is doing her best. She is not omniscient. She knows she is going to succeed this way, fail that way, and has a basically good feeling quality. She gets tired, depressed, angry, whatever. But she goes through things, she and the infant go through things together. They survive each other. They survive each other with a decent enough quality. The baby can forgive this mother and can enter into life in a state of communion, in a state of mutual give and take, mutual forgivability. Henry Elkin describes this in his papers, published in *The Psychoanalytic Review* and I recommend them (especially, 1957–8 and 1972).

In *The Psychotic Core* I bring out how dangerous omniscience is. On the negative side, it might be one of our most dangerous capacities because we think we know more about the other than we do, and we try to do things from that vantage point, which can be extremely destructive. If we are merely omnipotent, if we are merely a physical bully, a power bully, if we are merely a thug, someone is going to beat us up eventually. Insofar as the Bush group are bullies, are omnipotent, someone is going to beat them up eventually. Insofar as they are omniscient, insofar as the think they know what God wants and know more than everybody else, it is a real problem. You can correct a bully. If you are a prizefighter, sooner or later someone is going to knock you out. You know you are not omnipotent. You can be omnipotent only so long and someone knocks you out. If you are a king, someone is going to kill you or knock you out, here comes the next king. Omnipotence is correctable. Bullies are physically correctable. They have limits. To be omniscient, to think you know everything about the other or the world, or about how things should be—this is harder to disconfirm and correct. There is no way to disconfirm it. When you are acting from a viewpoint of omniscience, there is nothing in the physical world that can change your mind. You are not open to a change of mind. The second mother can't be changed. She knows what is right. She is intractable. This kind of omniscience about the baby's heart, the baby's being, the baby's body, hardens the baby. If someone is acting like they know more about you than you do, and are doing you harm from this knowledge, and misinterpreting your states and thinking something that is bad is good, and thinking something that is good is bad, and reversing everything according to their own pathology, their own negative omniscience, their own personality needs, then you harden and you can't forgive them. It just happens by itself. Again it is not a top-down thing; it is not a cognitive thing. It just happens. This unforgivability does very great damage to the personality and to the world. It begins with someone thinking they know more about you than they do. So beware, as analysts, of your own omniscience.

The baby knows more about some aspects of the mother than the mother knows herself. The baby sees, feels, and knows about the mother's state. Some of this knowledge, the mother can't acknowledge, the mother makes believe it is not so. 'What you see about me is not so. I only mean good things for you. I'm only interested in helping you. I'm only trying to make things good for you.' The baby sees something else perhaps, sees the mother's omniscience, or sees the mother's trickiness, or sees the mother's unconscious self perception, and the baby is stuck, is alone with this knowledge because it is not responded to. There is no place for it to go. There is no communion for this knowledge. So much of what psychoanalysis does in the beginning, at least in the first 5 years, is acknowledge the baby's knowledge of its environment, knowledge that the environment can't bear.

There is a phrase in English (is it a phrase in Korean too?) about a baby kicking. It's a life phrase. The phrase is 'alive and kicking.' The phrase is a common English phrase. The baby is alive and kicking.

These two worlds that I am describing, that Winnicott describes so vividly in his little picture of the baby kicking and how the kick is responded to, are presented as distinct, but of course in real life they are all mixed up. Real life is all mixed up. All our double attitudes are mixed up in a blender and often we can't tell one from the other. The tone keeps changing from moment to moment, day to day, year to year. All these changing qualities, tones, textures, spirits, have a cumulative effect for better or for worse. If one has this negative omniscience and is living by it, it's not good for oneself, for others or for society. It makes one a smaller person. It's an unfortunate thing. Struggling with and outgrowing omniscience is, in part, an evolutionary process. It's a long-range evolutionary process, millions of years perhaps. We're still very young.

Someone asked me to speak a little about what I mean by evolution and I mentioned that Bion has the notion that our minds grew up as survival minds. They handle how to survive in the physically dangerous world we once found ourselves in. We have a mind that is geared toward survival and it has survival mechanisms like hiding, tricking, being aggressive, and how you are change in order to benefit from the situation you are in, including predator-prey, fight-flight models. At about 500 years B.C. perhaps earlier, we begin to see an emergence across civilizations in different parts of the world of another concern, not just physical survival, but concern about the quality of survival and a new sense of the integrity of personality, going along with a nascent sense concerned with truth about our beings. Who and how we are, what kind of being we are. Interest in the quality of spirit, the tone of survival. Not just survival, but how we survive as persons. Issues about personal integrity begin a birth process.

So, we have a mind that has grown up to win, to survive, to stay alive any way it can, now dealing with issues of personal integrity. You see conflicts involved with it in the Bible. You see it in Greek plays. You can see it in other places too, e.g., the Egyptian Book of the Dead and in ancient transformation rites, and so on. An interest grows in quality of being, how life is for you, how life tastes for you, your growth as a person—not just fear, anger, aggression and living to survive. In literature, dying in order to protect integrity and quality of life becomes a theme. I'm not saying that you should die in order to protect your quality of life. Adaptation might be better or stay underground until conditions change. Maybe things will get better, maybe not. In any case, this issue arose and grew and Bion says our minds aren't well equipped for it. The idea of personal and communal truth, the idea of wholeness and issues of personal value and integrity—our mind is embryonic in capacity to work with the amazing flash of light it has produced.

One of the core things I would like to leave with you in this seminar is that we are all embryonic, that psychoanalysis is embryonic, that our minds are embryonic. Now you may or may not feel this because we have such casing. We have such baggage that we carry. Our personalities are formed this way or that way. It's like we can't live without our personalities but our personalities are also a burden. They form a casing around us. Still, we are embryonic inside our casing. What Bion and Winnicott offer is another way of looking at our evolutionary challenge. We have an evolutionary challenge to work with this new truth-mind, this person mind, the value of being a precious life form, a human being among other precious life forms on a precious earth all around us. We have a challenge to elaborate this feeling and learn how to work with it. Our embryonic mind and being. I'll be very happy if somehow nothing more gets communicated than to stay open to your own embryonic capacity and give it a chance to grow. Every little bit in your own life, no one else's life, your own life, every little bit of evolution you can do involving use, work, partnership with your embryonic psyche—every little bit is a contribution you can make to an evolutionary challenge. That is very much part of where we are today. I do feel every little bit counts.

I'd like to switch terms a bit. Instead of calling it mother one and mother two, the first mother and the second mother, call it what they are. They are two different attitudes, parts of the human capacity. We know the statistics. We have a worldwide epidemic in child abuse. And we have a worldwide epidemic in suicide. The two go together in some way because abuse isn't just in the family. It's also societal abuse. Spengler tells us that this is the age of economic man, of economic power. In our age, an economic age, money is more important than people, money is more important than human life, the financial is more important than human life. This is a crucial problem. It's a fact that is almost taken for granted. It's invisible. It's another kind of invisibility that financial power is more important than human life. Not only are lives destroyed by the power elite, but the latter's lives are destroyed as well. What it does to them as people is real. It has real consequences. That second mother, that second attitude, has to be addressed in an evolutionary way. And the struggle has to be thought of in thousands of years, not two, three, four decades. The Bible talks about a little seed, a little grain, a mustard seed, a mustard grain, a little light, a dim voice. The personality has so many tendencies, some of them are good, some of them not. So there's a long way to go. I wouldn't feel despairing if things don't come out ok tomorrow morning or the next day or the day after that. It's going to be a long haul, thousands of years for this kernel of truth to take root. The truth is that we are all important, all our lives are important. We all have our wondrous contributions to make whether they fit some external criteria or not. A very good essay to read is on normalcy, the feeling of normalcy, by Winnicott in *Psychoanalytic Explorations*. I write about it in *Toxic Nourishment*. He shows how conditioned the feeling of normalcy is. First he talks about a crippled child who, with a certain kind of mother, doesn't feel crippled, doesn't know it is crippled until it begins seeing itself from the outside. It has a vital spark. It has a vital feeling of oneself as a full being and doesn't start to feel like a crippled person until it comes up against other people who are evaluating his limitations. I write about it in *Toxic Nourishment* and show how a person can feel that a very toxic world, a very toxic atmosphere is normal and not build the equipment to go beyond that. So normal changes with the atmospheric condition that you are used to, that you have grown up in, that you know.

An analyst I talked about earlier, Dorothy Bloch (1977), wrote about unconscious maternal fantasies about infanticide, killing the baby. It's as if there is a situation in which the baby's life is too much for the mother. The mother can't bear it. Either the depressed mother, or the frightened mother, or the angry mother will have infanticide fantasies or wishes or urges. They might be conscious or they might be unconscious. Often they are unconscious or semiconscious. Dorothy Bloch attributed infantile depression to death wishes in the mother. And, indeed, in ancient Greek literature that is an important theme. You have infanticide. You have regicide. Killing the king, killing the baby, matricide, patricide and infanticide. Great Greek themes. Dorothy felt this is what often happens in the family with the mother and the baby. She attributes the depressive qualities of the infant to negative wishes of the mother. This might provide some basic understanding as to how Dorothy could support my life feeling without saying, "No." It somehow grew out of her view that she was working with unconscious wishes on the mother's part. I don't know if it was true in my case that my mother wished me dead or not. I think in my case it was more along the line that my mother was afraid of something, of the full quality of my being and was confused and didn't know what to do with me. Also however, death wishes would come out. She was frightened that she would drop me. Or she was frightened that she wouldn't feed me enough, that I would starve. I do feel in a deep way that our two primal dreads are starvation and suffocation, physically starving and suffocating as well as psychically. Perhaps that is as close to my mother's death wishes as I can get, a deep sense of starving and suffocating.

Corrective interactions, corrective actions happen all the time. We are always helping each other with these things. For me, it doesn't have to be a very big thing. Last night I was taking a walk after saying goodbye to Joon ho and Jae. And some people from the seminar came by. They were in good moods, good spirits. They waved and said hello and the baby me felt, 'Ah, there is a gleam in the mother's eyes.' A force for the good, a moment for the good, a little moment. Normally you don't think anything of it, but yes there was a good feeling. It was nice seeing them, nice of them saying hello. All this counts. Taking pictures with people during the break or talking with them. All that counts. All that adds to the good side. It's a corrective and it never stops. It's important. Even the way one says hello or slinks away. Every moment makes a tiny difference.

Well I keep going on and on about Winnicott. I didn't know that I was going to spend this much time on the Winnicottian situation. The overall picture is, 'Can we take each other? Can we survive each other? And with what quality, what tone? With what spirit? With what spontaneous feeling?' Winnicott is very much into emphasizing a spontaneous sense of things. Maybe more will come out in the afternoon when there will be more questions and answers and I will give a few cases too. I said, "questions and answers" but that is a language flaw, because I don't give answers. I don't know what the answers are, but I do try to respond. We will do that in the afternoon. Both Winnicott and Bion have gone farther than Melanie Klein's depiction of reparation. It's not that reparation isn't real, making up for your bad things. Winnicott is saying that reparation is not the thread he is interested in. That is not the spontaneous thread from the vital spark, from the going on being, through the transitional object, through the use of the object. No. He is saying that there is another thread, which is not about being guilty and making up for feeling guilty. There is another kind of spontaneity. Another joie de vivre that comes out of an élan, a feeling of a joy in life. It's not just that I want to make up for the bad things I've done. Yes, that's real and necessary, but not what Winnicott is tracking here. He is tracing a spontaneous thread of life that needs support. We have a chance to let this spontaneous life thread grow with every interaction we have.

With Winnicott, then, it is important how the other survives me. To what extent does the other survive me? How much of me can the other take? How much can I expect to be taken by the other? What are our limits in regard to being able to survive each other or to take each other's life force? It's an important evolutionary question in all kinds of ways. But we will have to let it go now because before the break I want to say something about Bion that is complementary to Winnicott. They go together.

An issue Bion brings up is the survival of our own murder. How do we survive our own murder? In the chapter, "A Basic Rhythm" in *The Sensitive Self*, there is a section called 'Bion's freeing murder', a murder that frees. There are a lot of kinds of murders. I'm not saying murder is necessarily a good thing, but it is part of who we are. We kill each other psychically. We are killers. All my work, in a sense, is about supporting faith in the face of our murders. In a nutshell, all my work is about supporting faith in face of what is inimical about ourselves in life. If one can somehow find the right spot, the right attitude, everything looks different. It all begins to be usable. It begins to be workable more or less. So in his book *Cogitations* (p. 104), Bion writes about being murdered, then being all right. You get killed, then you are all right. If you are going to have a relationship with anyone, you are going to have to prepare to be murdered. We kill each other in a relationship. And the trick is to be all right after you get murdered. Maybe not in five minutes, maybe not in two hours. But sooner or later one comes through being murdered and is all right.

It is important to get the support that is needed in order to let this rhythm click in. Now this may not sound right to you because Bion is so hard for many of you. But Bion is about supporting the psyche, supporting the person in face of his insupportable psyche, giving support to the person, being almost an auxiliary dream worker, or an auxiliary semi-psyche. Support the person in face of the psyche that the person cannot support. In this case, support in undergoing being murdered and then being all right, a cycle, a sequence, a rhythm. How we achieve this is a necessary question if we are going to live with some decent quality with each other. We are all going to have to learn to be murdered and to be all right if we are going to have a good quality relationship. The other has to learn to be killed by us and be OK, and we have to learn to be killed by the other and be OK. Part of the idea of the other surviving destruction means the other survives his own murder. This is a basic capacity that Bion is talking about. It is sort of the reverse of Winnicott. But it is a capacity that is implicit in Winnicott's use of the object formulation. The idea that the other survives us means that the other has to survive being murdered in certain instances, at certain times. And has to survive it well. Certain mothers do this—they go under, they come back. I'm very open with my patients about this, if I think they can take it. Later today I'll give you an incident that almost did not work out, that is on the edge. A woman I work with was not able to take something I said. I let down prematurely and a disaster almost happened.

Here is an excerpt from *The Sensitive Self* about aspects of the basic rhythm I am touching:

> *For Bion murder is part of psychic birth, a kind of being murdered into life, a process of discovery. One learns it is possible to survive murder one is sure one cannot survive, a learning necessary for growth. As aliveness grows toward an apex, murder comes to meet it. If one holds back out of fear, murder grows in menace, an impassable barrier. Arrested or avoided death becomes a stagnant element in life. Bion invites us to practice getting murdered, ultimately being enlivened by it. Murder is a passageway, a divide: one cannot feel all right if one cannot come through it. Or, rather, coming through it enables one to feel all right in a new way, a way that encompasses more of what one dreaded. The quality of self and personality feels different depending on whether, or to what extent, one is a pre- or post-murdered being.*
>
> *The knack or "feel" of coming through each other's impact needs nurturing. Bion emphasizes coming through the Other's destructiveness, Winnicott stresses the Other coming through self's destructiveness—two profiles of a dual capacity. We come through ourselves and each other and the quality of coming through depends, partly, on how well we kill and are killed. There is an art of coming through impacts, a capacity easily abused and exploited, but important if we are to work well together* (p. 31).

* * *

Afternoon session: Where we are: Clinical reflections and loose threads to pull

One thought I had and wanted to pass along was about the word "sensing", to sense. A lot of what we do is to sense. It's a rich word in English. The way Freud and Bion use it makes it even richer. Freud talks about the ego being an organ of psychic sensing, psychic perception. What he suggests when he talks about the ego as a sense organ is complex, has many levels of meaning. It's not just about sensory data, although it includes the latter. Sensory experience helps make us feel alive, sentient. Freud also means sense as meaning, but also something else: psychic sensing. A kind of sensing not just with ears, nose, eyes, mouth, skin, although, perhaps a kind of psychic skin is involved. But a kind of psychic sensing as when one senses a mood, an atmosphere. What organ senses the "feel" of a place, the taste of a person? That is the kind of sensing psychoanalysis uses most of all, a kind of sensing of what's going on.

Some people call it intuition. It's not just intuition, it's also something else. Animals have this sensing. They sense the atmosphere, the feelings of the atmosphere. They smell, they feel, they sense the fear, they sense the danger. In psychoanalysis it's still broader. You sense emotional states of all sorts that aren't visible, or are barely visible, or that the patient may not even know he has. Part of a model for work, part of what I am trying to convey is that because of our ability to sense the psyche, a kind of psychic sensing, we may spontaneously at times unveil for patients senses that they didn't know they had, and that become important to them. I was thinking of an instance of this the other day when I was talking to Joon ho about an example that Emanuel Ghent (1990), a New York analyst, gives in one of his papers. His patient was lying on the couch and he gets up at some point and brings over a blanket and puts it on her. He sensed that she was cold and she didn't say anything about it. Once he gave her the blanket, she realized that she was cold. It's as if she didn't know she was cold and needed warmth until he supplied warmth that she didn't know she needed. Once she experienced this warmth, she realized she needed it. This is a physical thing and it is an emotional thing. It opened up room to exchange affect that couldn't have happened otherwise. This is a little but dramatic example of the ability to sense another's state. Sometimes it's possible to do something gracefully, or tactfully, in correspondence with that state, in coherence with that state in an unshaming way. In a way that enables the patient to link up with a need or feeling that they come to value. 'I do need warmth.'

I once referred a child of a parent I was treating to a child therapist who was a self-psychologist. I thought since this person was a self-psychologist, he would be warm and empathic. Within a month of the child beginning treatment, the mother indicated that this child was getting worse. He was starting to do bizarre things and write troubling things. It sounded like he was losing affect or losing a link with his affective self. I became quite concerned and spoke with the therapist and we started talking about how we work with children. I asked him if he uses toys, because I hadn't heard about toys or playing in the sessions. He revealed that the toys are in the closet and that the room is otherwise bare, although a nice room. He has a pad and paper that the child could use and toys if the child opens the closet door. This child did not open the closet door. So the child never found the toys. The therapist felt it was up to the child to explore, to find what he needed. The model was somehow; you let the child find what he needs. Well it struck me as bizarre, as starving the patient and not at all supportive to let this kid stew in his own juices. Maybe he was too afraid or too inhibited to open a door that was shut. Or maybe he was respectful of boundaries and felt no need to go into the closet. I supported the mother in taking him out of treatment and referred him to a warmer, kinder therapist and then things went along OK. The "closet door" model was very different from Emanuel Ghent's, a little meshugana as they say in Yiddish, depriving. The therapist had his rationale for it, his theory, and went by his own particular book. He was not the kind of therapist who would give a cold patient a blanket if she didn't ask for it.

How does one honour a patient one wants to kill or one can't stand? Years ago I wrote a paper, now a chapter in *The Electrified Tightrope* (1993), called 'Working with unwanted patients', patients you don't want to be with, that disgust or repulse you, who make you hate them or bring you to a point you can't bear. Very often in New York people would talk about what to do if Hitler came to see you. How would you treat him? My wife currently has someone who hates just about everybody. He especially hates Jews. He hates minority groups. I don't know whom he doesn't hate. My wife has been with him for about three years and his personality drives her crazy. He spends the time viciously hating everybody. Yet they are still together. God only knows what is going to happen. I remember one day she risked being a little more herself and said to him, "You know you sound like a Nazi." The next week he comes in and said, "I guess I do sound like a Nazi." He wasn't exactly proud of sounding like a Nazi but wasn't apologetic about it either. It seemed syntonic to him. The therapy continues and we don't know what is going to happen. He is alive. He hasn't killed himself. He gets a little more work than he used to. It's hard to say what is happening. But I can feel something is happening and keep supporting her in this. That's part of what therapists do—we are civil insofar as we can be to people we can't stand, because these people hate themselves. These people have been hated and became grandiose as a way of escaping suicide. They are in a state of emotional starvation and are this far away from death. Sometimes we are the only thing, the only object that separates them from that. Sometimes you may think they are better off dead, let them kill themselves, just let them die. It's odd to say, but we grow through sustaining this. We grow, we gain, the therapist gains in the long run by sustaining such a situation with the faith that all is not lost.

Years ago I used to joke that therapy is good for society because it keeps guys like me off the street, gives me something to do. And this Nazi that sees my wife, it keeps him off the street, so to speak. It keeps him from doing worse things. Here he has a victim, a nice warm victim, warm blooded, not cold blooded. He can spew out all his hatred. It's an awful situation. You have to be invisible. You have to get into the invisible. I am sure this never happened in his life that he should be spewing out all this terrible cold hatred, all this evil stuff, all this bile, to a warm hearted person. It doesn't exist and here it is happening. It is a strange juxtaposition. Maybe this is the best he can do to get close to someone, to have a warm hearted victim, someone who is forced to stay with him for forty five minutes, once a week and hear all this shit. It gives him a place to go. It gives him something to look forward to. 'Ah. I can see Betty and vomit all this stuff out.' It's like he saves it for her. He doesn't do it when he is working. He doesn't do it when he is walking down the street or going to the market. He saves it for her. She is becoming his place to be awful. And it has a social function and it has a personal function. I think in a case like this a lot of what we do is play for time. It doesn't matter what you say or what you do. If you want to do something nasty, do something nasty. I once had a so-called chronic psychotic patient. They called him chronic schizophrenic in those days. This psychotic patient smiled at everything. Everything made him happy. I was a young therapist at the time so I had ambition,

I wanted the patients to get better. I didn't know much better than that then. So I would press for some action. I told my supervisor I'd like to try to poke him a little and get some aggression out of him. I'd like to do something to get some fight, some anger out of him. He said, "You can do whatever you like." And he meant whatever I do, nothing is going to come out of this man. He is going to be nice and deny any kind of feeling. He is going to go on and on like that. What you learn in situations like this is to play for time. Wait it out. It doesn't matter what you say or do. And sooner or later, God be willing, there is a cumulative impact. You are getting impacted by this awful person, and it is toxic. It is not good for you. A lot of stuff that happens to us is not really healthy, not really good. You have to do other things to balance it. But remember, you're not only getting this bad impact from such a situation, you are also unconsciously impacting the other person. You are having an impact on the other person although it may not be visible yet.

I'm not advising you to say or do nothing. That would be like the situation of starvation that I described with the child, where all the toys were behind a closed door awaiting the child's curiosity and activity that were not forthcoming. I'm not advising that. But I would not have any great hopes in any particular thing I might say. That is not where the action is. The action is not verbal. The action is in a non-verbal place. We have to say things whenever we feel the need to keep the person interested. We are all smart and learned enough to think of interesting things to say now and then that the patient hasn't thought of, and give him something to think about. That used to be called psychoanalytic interpretation or understanding. It may or may not be useful, but it does help us play for time.

Many of you have read in Winnicott that when he was older he said that he occasionally says something just to let the patient know he is there. The patient shouldn't feel that he is too abandoned, the patient shouldn't get to the Z point. Winnicott knew that a certain kind of waiting and sensing and letting the unconscious speak was the important thing. He knew that the affective atmosphere in the room counted most.

In 1977 or 1978, Bion was in New York to give a week long seminar for a good psychoanalytic institute. The institute had a strong, traditional, well organized training program. They had some Winnicottians. Saul Tuttman, who looked a little like Ferenczi, set up programs that featured British analysts. Saul was one of the early teachers of object relations in New York City and invited Bion, who I had been reading and started teaching. I began teaching him as a way of learning him. He was not your usual presenter. He doesn't use notes, doesn't look at papers. Just sits and talks for about twenty or thirty minutes and then responds to questions. One night someone asked, "Don't you ever use psychoanalytic theory? Don't you ever use Freudian theory? Don't you ever use psychoanalytic interpretations?" And he said, "Thank God for Freud. He's great when you're tired."

To try to get the most out of such a rare visit, I had some sessions with him, which turned out to be important. He helped me get married. I found him extremely supportive. I couldn't believe it. He was a tall, formal Edwardian British man. He was old but with a straight back, he used to be an athlete, a swimmer. Kind of formal and yet I felt an instant intimacy with him. I didn't know exactly why. And then I realized at once. It was because he looked afraid and he was mirroring me. I think he was mirroring me at that moment. His face took on my soul configuration and he was a big man, much bigger than I. He suddenly somehow became under me, to stand under. It happened spontaneously, instantly. It was very fast and externally I thought he sort of looked like a bug, kind of joyless. Yet in our conversation he was very open. I can't go through all the details of the conversation. It is still vivid with me thirty years later. I can't believe it is that long. They were packed sessions. He didn't let me die. He didn't let me suffocate or starve. His sensing did everything—his unconscious sensing did everything. He brought up a number of things I didn't bring up. I didn't bring them up, he did. He said just out of the blue, "You know, marriage is not what you think it is." I was not married, in my forties, never married. Oh my God! I was scared to death of any such thought. It's entrapment. He said, "You know it's not what you think it is. It's having someone to speak truth to, to mitigate the severity to yourself." That was all he said at the moment. "Marriage is having someone to speak truth to who can mitigate the severity to yourself." That was it. I got married within two years. The way it happened, it just helped free me. I thought about it and thought about it and Jesus maybe I've been all wrong about something and it caused a kind of revolution. He did a number of things out of the blue that anticipated my needs without my saying them that had a life impact. Not everyone can do that. I don't know if I can do that. Sometimes, yes. I wouldn't count on it most of the time.

I think of one life changing thing I did manage to do many years ago. I wrote about it in 'Working with unwanted patients.' (IJPA [1977] and *The Electrified Tightrope,* also see *The Psychotic Core*) A lucky hit, a lucky moment early in my clinical work. I moved from working with disturbed children in treatment centers and schools, to working in a clinic with adults as well. The man I am thinking of looked pinched, as if his whole body was contorted and deformed. I saw that it wasn't a physical deformity. It was body tension, body strangulation. He was being strangulated, suffocated by what Wilhelm Reich calls body armoring. His character, his armoring was pinching himself, strangling himself. He was in his thirties, disabled in his ability to work and take care of himself, living with his mother. I liked being with him, I don't know why.

Ever since I was a little boy, I would befriend kids other kids didn't like. I'd be with kids they liked too, but I always had a feeling for the ones who were made fun of, who were ridiculed and felt really bad about themselves. I would befriend them. I was moved. They would move me and I didn't know why, very like the man I just mentioned. When I first started doing therapy I felt like a fish in water. It was natural. It was like I found an atmosphere I could live in. It wasn't training, it wasn't forced or anything outside. It reminds me of something Erroll Garner, an instinctive piano player said. Garner didn't read music. He was basically self-taught, picked things out of the air (maybe also inner air). He could play any song in any key. He drove his bass player crazy because the bass player never knew what he was going to do next. He would pop into another key or tempo if he was so inspired or start another song. A fun kind of crazy. Someone asked him, "How do you do it? You don't read music. You never got taught." Garner said, "How do you get horny?" He just does it. I guess I felt something like that when I started doing sessions. A lot of learning, though, went into it over the years. Garner never stopped growing. The kinds of chords and sequences he played later in his life were far more developed than those he played earlier.

Well, back to the story of the pinched strangulated man who was living with his mother and not able to do anything in life. One day he comes in and I'm looking at him and he is looking at me and he is chatting about his miserable life and good things but mostly bad things. I don't even think and my mouth opens and I say "It seems you can't stop living in your mother's asshole." And it was like a 'pop.' Within two months he had his own apartment. One other thing about him. What prompted the remark was that he often spoke about smelling shit everywhere. The world smelled of shit. No matter where he went the world smelled shitty, literally. And that somehow led to my offhand remark, "It seems you can't stop living in your mother's asshole." I can't say why I said that then and not before. It just happened. It was one of the unusual times when a particular remark I made had a big impact. Usually, work in the trenches is cumulative and gradual. Of course, our background together, our time together and our feeling together supported a remark like that. But I would not have predicted my saying what I did and surely would not have predicted the result. It was very dramatic because the smell of shit went away right after the remark. It took him a moment to realize it. He had been smelling shit practically all his life and after that remark he was actually able to breathe without smelling it. I thought, 'Oh my God. I wish I could do this all the time.'

As I said the other day, dosing things out is so important. You don't have to do it all at once. You shouldn't try to do more than you can. Here is an example, a patient of Susan Deri. She brought this patient up in Bion's seminar. Susan wrote a good book on Winnicott and was a highly experienced, creative analyst. Her patient was what they called chronic schizophrenic at that time. Over the years she helped him get his own apartment and he began to sustain himself through work he could do and began to take care of himself. This took a long time, many years. Hymen Spotnitz, a psychiatrist-analyst in New York, used to say that it takes at least five years of therapy with a schizophrenic patient before real changes start. I think it can be longer than that but it was a relief as a younger man for me to hear that. If you don't see any changes at first just keep at it. Don't give up. Don't lose the faith. So then, Susan's patient comes into the office and announces that he wants love. He wants to fall in love. He wants a sweetheart. Well, Susan didn't know what to make of this one. She didn't really expect it to be possible. She saw his emotional potential as very limited. Such love didn't happen for her. She was a grown lady. She had two sons, both successful professionals.

She had no love life. And here this chronic schizophrenic wants a love life. So she humours him. She supports him. She is still there for him but she is also afraid that he is going to be hurt and she doesn't know how he is going to handle the hurt because he is reaching for the impossible.

The miracle happened. It could be after twenty years of therapy. He fell in love and the woman fell in love with him and they got married. And they went on a honeymoon and he was absolutely glorious. He never gave up on himself. The therapist had given up on him. It was wondrous. He died on his honeymoon, heart attack. His heart burst. His heart burst with joy and he died. And Susan felt helpless in face of that and kept on telling the story until she got used to living with it, she felt so guilty. I suspect a far-reaching problem lies in this story. A question about resources, whether or not we have the resources to support psychic growth. To what extent? How far can we go? So much of therapy involves building up resources in order to support what growth is possible. How much aliveness can we take? We build up resources as we go or what we do is lost. This may be related to dosing therapy out in accord with what one's system can stand (see *Psychic Deadness*). Yet things happen spontaneously, for better and worse. We are not in control of psychic reality. We are not sure what we do when we tinker around. We go by a certain feel for things and hope it comes out OK. Analysis is based on and works through a kind of faith. We try to partner the vast resources that support and threaten us.

There are two cases I would like to share from recent practice. This happened last month. It's a little incident to give some feel for how flexible psychoanalysis can be now, if you need support for finding your own way. The kinds of things you can say depend on what your reflective imagination brings up, or what your heart brings up, or what your soul or mind brings up. I'd like to help support what comes from you and urge you to keep on using yourself. Keep on doing, keep on using, and the sensing thing takes on a life of its own. It develops. It undergoes development.

A man, Sam, comes in, a once chronically alone person. He married and fathered a child during the time I have been with him, many years. He was used to being alone before marriage, worked alone, lived alone, isolated. He worked from his own apartment, his own boss in his little place.

He met someone who also was isolated and they had to learn how to be together, learn how to make adjustments to each other's personalities. Both of them were former alcoholics and both were free from alcohol for a long time. One day he comes to session with the following dream. He has a poetic and strong spiritual side. His dream is about a dead friend whom he hadn't seen in decades. His friend died some time ago and he hadn't thought about him for a long time and all of a sudden he dreams about him. We will call his friend William. In the dream, William is alive and well. In real life he had been an irascible, self-destructive life figure. He was filled with life but it was self-destructive. His life feeling worked against him. If you have any doubts how aliveness can work against you, think of the beginning of Western literature. It begins with war because of an erotic theft. Someone steals someone's woman and the Greeks and the Trojans start fighting about it. Life gets you into trouble, the life feeling, aliveness can get you into trouble. Anyway, William died prematurely. He had been an alcoholic too and he didn't survive his own destructive life drive. When Sam was talking about William, I had a feeling that William appeared to him so that, I don't know how to put it exactly, so that his dream can honor him. So that this dream can honour William's life, William's failed life. In the dream William is looking much better. Now ordinarily I would understand that something in Sam has changed and is now appearing much better, less self-destructive. A growth that appears as William getting better. That often happens in a dream e.g., a parent who is an awful parent will look better in a dream. It may mean that something in oneself is getting better. The parent within is getting better. One's feelings are getting better. One is less self-hating. But I didn't say that.

Something else came out of my mouth. What came out of my mouth was that William came into the dream so that the dream can honor him. "You are honoring William's life. The dream is honoring William's life. And it's your job to honor the dream." Why this thought? Where did it come from? A dream to honour William's life, a dream to honour. Not a usual therapy thought for me, but I shared it with Sam. Sam sat feelingly, reflectively. When he spoke, he said that he felt something complete with the acceptance of William coming to be with him, to see him and be seen. That was the episode. It may not sound like much, but something happened.

Question: Can you say more about what you mean by honouring the dream? Do you mean that *you* were honouring the dream?

Yes, I felt I was honouring the dream, that the dream came to be honored. But more, I felt the dream itself was honouring William's life, and that we were asked to honour William's life through the intermediary of the dream. Sometimes guilt prevents one from seeing someone's essence. Perhaps the dream showed an essential William and gave him honour. And that our job, mine and especially Sam's, was to honour this transmission. It led to a sense of William's life as a whole, a deep appreciation, a deep reconciliation, acceptance. What Bion might call at-onement. What I wouldn't want lost is the sense that the dream gave honor to his friend's life and that it was Sam's job to honour the dream. It wasn't simply me honouring the dream though I certainly did. The dream meaning was that the patient had to honor what his dream produced and that had a momentarily completing effect.

I would like to share one more episode. Something I feel deeply about and that frightened me at the time. It involved a woman who had a lot of therapy. A sensitive, bright, hard working woman. She tended to have affairs with her therapists and finally found a male therapist who did not do this. It was the breakup of this therapy that sent her to me.

Her therapist was very experienced and highly regarded, the only other analyst beside myself who did not sleep with her. I appreciated how she and therapists could fall into sleeping together. She had a needy appeal that made you feel like falling into a warm boundless sea. There is much to be said about what was driving a need for special intimacy but we will not do justice to this today.

Although her last therapist did not sleep with her, he made allowances that went beyond his usual frame and conduct. He and she created a situation in which—at last—her maternal needs were being met. The good mother is finally giving her what she always wanted. This spiraled into his giving her as many sessions as she wanted and phone calls between sessions. He was the supplier of needs, redressing all her injuries, all her deprivation, all her bad mothering. He was the cure. Then one day he breaks off treatment. A lot of factors went into this abrupt ending. His moralistic, psychoanalytic superego rose up and he told her, "This isn't psychoanalysis that we are doing! If you want to go farther than what we have done, you have to use the couch!" They were sitting face to face and she didn't want to use the couch. She was in her own way very fragile but used to weathering her fragility, a tough tenacity in her fragility.

They had been seeing each other six days a week and sometimes they would talk on the phone on Sunday. Then he tells her he had a dream of her and in the dream they were doing something sexual. He told the dream to his wife and his wife didn't want him to see her. So he is telling her use the couch, but my wife doesn't want me to see you. One morning he showed up in his pajamas. He forgot about the session. He opened the door when it rang. I don't know what he thought, maybe he expected the newspaper man. And there he stood in his bed clothes. And she freaked out. She didn't know what to do.

To make a long story short, his behaviour forced her to leave therapy. He created a situation in which she couldn't stay. This is one way we get rid of patients. We create situations in which they can't stay. At least maybe it feels to them that they made the decision to leave us. That has some merit. But she did not feel good about leaving. It was not what she wanted to do, not what she hoped would happen. She felt forced to leave. She felt horrible about leaving, the hope of goodness suddenly dashed. She had a taste of the goodness she always wanted and now it was smashed, taken away from her, withdrawn and she was back to being as anxious, as depressed as she ever was, in some ways worse, for now goodness was shattered.

This is not an unheard of problem or danger in our field, to elicit dependency in the patient and smash it, not be able to come through. You elicit a need you can not support or lack resources to work with well. You elicit a need or a wish in the patient that you think that you are going to gratify but you really don't have ability to do that and you end up cutting off supplies and the patient goes downhill. I've seen this happen with therapists of diverse "schools", eliciting dependency that one lacks resources to meet or work with and cutting it off. It is much better to dose it out. Don't try to do too much. Don't ask too much from yourself or the patient. Do it naturally. There is a double rhythm made up of dependent and independent tendencies. You play one against the other, give each something of its due. Let all tendencies have their say, support the various tendencies that want to have a voice. It balances out. An interplay of tendencies.

In the introduction to *Psychic Deadness,* I give another example of the danger I am touching. A woman went to a highly regarded analyst who elicited dependency as a supposed antidote for emotional starvation. She became seriously anorexic, stopped eating and got skinnier and skinner, down to 80 pounds. She looked like a corpse. He got frightened and bolted. He didn't want a suicide or death on his hands and stopped treatment. Kicked her out, just like that. The excuse he gave: "I didn't know you were that ill. If I had known you were that ill, I wouldn't have accepted you to start with." Our field is filled with horror stories—and many good stories as well.

I am in danger of ranting about what can be at stake in making emotional promises that can't be fulfilled and the effects of this on a person's life. Emotional promises can have disastrous outcomes. Best not to make hidden promises. Never make promises and don't be over-attached to any one theory, to any one point of view. All the views—if they are authentic—express different parts of human nature. Don't be overly attached to your own way of doing things. See what unfolds with each person and what unfolds with you.

Back to the patient I was talking about. The shock, the trauma of her therapist breaking up with her left her in tatters, broken, and precipitated a search for a new therapist and she found her way to me. This reminds me—another story—of a person who was rejected by her last three therapists. A very angry and very smart woman. I liked her but did not know whether or not she was going to stay with me. She ended up staying awhile but eventually left. She had a very high functioning job that affected many people yet suffered from a fathomless depression. She was on an array of medications and had been for many years.

One day I get a call from her last analyst. He complained that she had not paid him and did not respond to his repeated bills. Well, I listened but it was not up to me to solicit payment from the patient for him. It was hard enough hanging in there with her for the time she stayed with me. Bills were never an issue with us. She paid on time.

Eventually, she stopped coming. Several months later I again received a call from her previous therapist, this one in sympathy. He was sorry to hear my patient killed herself. He received his latest bill back with the envelope marked "Deceased." Something sank in me. She certainly could kill herself, she was so depressed, had so many pills. I didn't know what to think. This was news to me. Did she kill herself? I was stymied. First this man calls me as if his bill is the most important thing in the world. Now he sympathizes with me over a massive failure. I began to agonize over it and told my wife a former patient may have killed herself. Did she leave therapy so she could kill herself?

Then one morning after a night of sleeping and thinking, I wake up and go to the phone and call her and there is no answer. And then someone picks up the phone and clicks it, hangs up. A few minutes later, I get a call and the person hangs up. So I knew she was alive. This was a non-verbal communication. We don't know ahead of time what form of communication we will receive. This was a new form of communication for me. But I knew inside immediately, she is alive. She is just stiffing him. So about two months later I get a call from this former analyst and he is furious. He is just so angry. He said, "Did you know that she is still alive?" Inside of course I knew and I said, "Gosh, Lenny." It was beautiful—I don't know what to call such transmissions. Some call it ego. It is much deeper than that.

Well, I had better get back to the case I tried to begin with. I see we are running out of time so I will try to make it short. The woman, decimated by her last therapy—she used the word "broken"—stayed with me a long time, many years, as long as she needed. Little by little, she has gotten her own mind back. She began to have more faith in herself, saw things could be different. She was hopeful about starting a new phase of her life. I want to speak a little bit of one of her recent sessions, one we had soon before my coming here.

We were together a long time so we went through a lot. One session I stupidly thought I could let my guard down. I was thinking of coming to Seoul to be with you today and that had something to do with it. So I blame you too. I made an error of judgment. I indulged myself in the session. She was talking about important things for her. My mind drifted to this trip I was about to take. It is a big thing for me because I don't accept many of the invitations I get but something in me said, "I want to do this one." Maybe it was going to a different part of the world. Maybe it was my interest in Taoism and Buddhism. Maybe it was because I don't have much time left on this earth and this was something different. So I'm sitting thinking about the trip. And I worry about the trip. I am accident prone. If I go on a trip, the chances are I am going to get hurt. And if I don't get hurt, the chances are I am going to get sick. I am worried about picking up some bug. Is the food on the street safe? Can I drink the water? I'm worried about getting hurt and I'm worried about getting sick. And I am sitting there thinking about the trip. What is it going to be like? What do I want? Why am I doing this? As the time came for the trip I became more afraid and less interested in going. So I was sitting there absorbed in all this. I wasn't thinking about her. I was drifting.

Out of the blue, she asks me, "What are you thinking?" She urges me to tell her and for a moment it felt like I could do that. "Well," I say. "I was thinking about a trip I am going to take." So I let my guard down and made this indulgence. I don't know what made me think I could or should tell her, but I told her that I am thinking about this trip. Maybe a false sense of intimacy made me feel I could do it (an adumbrated version of the intimacy that was acted out and wounded in past therapies). And she went crazy. She blew. She was furious. She started attacking me with the same old fury I knew for years. She couldn't believe it. Here she was telling these deep things, these true things, and I was thinking about a trip. How could I not be paying attention to her?

It's a little like a Bion vignette we did. Things are good then something goes off. That finished it! It is very similar. A kind of life long primary maternal preoccupation. Winnicott describes a time, in the first three months, when the mother's attention is mostly riveted on the baby. Her being is tied up with the baby. In my patient's case, that maternal preoccupation has been wounded and one is attached to getting that all one's life long. We want to give it to each other in one way or another. It undergoes development and becomes much more refined.

Anyway, she demands that I comment on her life and comment on what she has been telling me about her life and I am unable to. I am paralyzed. I go blank. I have nothing to say about what she has been saying. As a matter of fact I feel put upon because we've talked about this stuff a million times and she is on the verge of doing something about it and now she wants me to say the same old thing when I'm about to do something different too. I don't know what to do and I say nothing. She couldn't believe that I was going to leave the session like this so she gives me an assignment. She demands that I think about what happened for the next session and find out my motives, my unconscious reasons why I acted this way. I am supposed to analyze myself and come in and tell her what I learned.

I thought about it during the week and nothing came to me. I had nothing to say for myself. I wasn't sure myself why I did it. All I knew is that I gave in to a moment's indulgence and paid the price. So the next session began with her asking me what I understood. What did I learn? What did I come up with? And I hadn't come up with anything satisfactory. Nothing that would be like an interpretation or an understanding the way she wanted. But something did happen. One night in the middle of the night, I suddenly felt something more deeply. I don't know what. I felt our plight more deeply. I felt she was asking me for something and I was blind. I didn't have the goods. I didn't have what was required and I felt a deep grief, a deep sorrow, a deep sadness that something tragic was happening that was deeper than what seemed to be going on.

So I felt OK about the session that was coming. I wasn't as afraid anymore because I was feeling something deeply but I was unsure of what I was feeling. I felt it was important. Very often we feel something and it is important and we don't know what it is. Don't think too hard about what it is. Honour that something. So I didn't know what it was but I was glad I was feeling something more deeply and I was able to see her.

When I failed to come up with an interpretation about my behaviour, she starts talking about something off with us, something is off with us, between her and me. And something is off, she says, in the various parts of her life. In her marriage, in her work, with her friends. She says she wanted me to fix it and fix her and she wants to fix her husband, fix her family, fix her mother, fix her sisters, fix her father. She wanted it all to be fixed. She wanted life to be fixed. Something broken in life. She wanted to make it unbroken. And I look at her and the feeling speaks, I don't speak. Finally words come out of the feeling and I say, "I am broken." And she says, "I want to fix you." And I say, "I can't be fixed" and profoundly meant it. "Whether you stay or go, I can't be fixed. Your staying or leaving can't fix me, no matter what you do." It's true. She weeps, she cries. I say to her after she weeps a bit. "Always trying to fix things, fix the brokenness, the brokenness that is part of life. Yet in the center of my broken heart," me, I am talking about me. "In the center of my broken heart there is a golden radiant point."

In the next session she comes in and I can see the change, a profound feeling in her. She was being herself. She was being also free not heavy. She felt better, she felt good again. We went through something together. What a deep relief we both felt. She told me something happened on the way to the office that day. Something very touching. There is a synagogue around the corner from my office. She is not Jewish. On the temple there is a saying from one of the prophets, Micah. The saying engraved on the temple is, 'What does God want of you but do justice, love mercy, and walk humbly with thy God.' She said she never saw that before on the way to my office. She never read, she never heard, such beautiful words. She said this a number of times, "I never heard such beautiful words." The whole room softened. We sat quietly together, uplifted by shared ripples of this moment.

REFERENCES

Bion, W.R. (1992). *Cogitations*. London: Karnac Books.
Bion, W.R. (2000). *The Paris Seminar*.
   http://www.psychoanalysis.org.uk/bion78.htm
Bion, W.R. (1980). *Bion in New York and Sao Paulo*. London: Karnac Books.
Bion, W.R. (2005). *The Tavistock Seminars*. London: Karnac Books.
Bion, W.R. (2005). *The Italian Seminars*. London: Karnac Books.
Bion, W.R. (1994). *Clinical Seminars and Other Works*. London: Karnac Books.
Bloch, D. (1977). *So the Witch Won't Eat Me: Fantasy and the Child's Fear of Infanticide*. Lanham, MD: Jason Aronson.
Eigen, M. (1977). On working with 'unwanted' patients. IJPA, 58: 109–121.
Eigen, M. (1986). *The Psychotic Core*. London: Karnac Books, 2004.
Eigen, M. (1992). *Coming Through the Whirlwind*. Wilmette, Ill: Chiron Publications.
Eigen, M. (1993). *The Electrified Tightrope*. A. Phillips ed. London: Karnac Books, 2004.
Eigen, M. (1996). *Psychic Deadness*. London: Karnac Books, 2004.
Eigen, M. (1998). *The Psychoanalytic Mystic*. London: Free Association Books.

Eigen, M. (2002). *Rage*. Middletown, CT: Wesleyan University Press.
Eigen, M. (2004). *The Sensitive Self*. Middletown, CT: Wesleyan University Press.
Eigen, M. (2005). *Emotional Storm*. Middletown, CT: Wesleyan University Press.
Eigen, M. (2006). Age of Psychopathy. http://www.psychoanalysis-and-therapy.com/human_nature/eigen/pref.html
Eigen, M. (2007). *Feeling Matters*. London: Karnac Books.
Eigen, M. (2009). *Flames From the Unconcious: Trauma, Madness and Faith*. London: Karnac Books.
Elkin, H. (1958). On the origin of the self. *The Psychoanalytic Review*, 45: 57–76.
Elkin, H. (1972). On selfhood and the development of ego structures in infancy. The Psychoanalytic Review, 59: 389–416.
Freud, S. (1911). Psychoanalytic notes on an autobiographical account of a case of paranoia (dementia paranoids). Standard Edition, 12: 3–82.
Freud, S. (1921). Group Psychology and the analysis of the Ego. Standard Edition, 18: 65–143.
Ghent, E. (1990). Masochism, submission, surrender: Masochism as a perversion of surrender. Contemporary Psychoanalysis, 26: 141–207.
Klein, M. (1946). Notes on some schizoid mechanisms. In: M. Klein, P. Heimann, S. Isaacs & J. Riviere (Eds), *Developments in Psychoanalysis*. London: Hogarth Press (1952), pp. 292–320.
Klein, M. (1957). *Envy and Gratitude*. New York: Basic Books.
Lothane, Z. (1992). *In Defense of Schreber: Soul Murder and Psychiatry*. New York: Routledge.
Winnicott, D.W. (1990). *Human Nature*. New York: Routledge.
Winnicott, D.W. (1992). *Psychoanalytic Explorations*. C. Winnicott, R. Shepherd and M. Davis (Eds). Cambridge, MA: Harvard University Press.

Made in the USA
Monee, IL
03 May 2026

49438599R00056